Jefferson & Atatürk

Major Concepts in Politics and Political Theory

Garrett Ward Sheldon
General Editor

Vol. 21

PETER LANG
New York • Washington, D.C./Baltimore • Boston • Bern
Frankfurt am Main • Berlin • Brussels • Vienna • Oxford

Garrett Ward Sheldon

Jefferson & Atatürk

Political Philosophies

PETER LANG
New York • Washington, D.C./Baltimore • Boston • Bern
Frankfurt am Main • Berlin • Brussels • Vienna • Oxford

Library of Congress Cataloging-in-Publication Data

Sheldon, Garrett Ward.
Jefferson and Atatürk: political philosophies / by Garrett Ward Sheldon.
p. cm. — (Major concepts in politics and political theory; vol. 21)
Includes bibliographical references and index.
1. Jefferson, Thomas, 1743–1826—Political and social views. 2. Atatürk, Kemal, 1881–1938—Political and social views. 3. United States—Politics and government—1775–1783. 4. United States—Politics and government—1783–1809. 5. Turkey—Politics and government—1918–1960. I. Title. II. Series.
E332.2.S538 973.4'6'0922—dc21 99-087266
ISBN 978-0-8204-4977-7
ISSN 1059-3535

Bibliographic information published by **Die Deutsche Nationalbibliothek**.
Die Deutsche Nationalbibliothek lists this publication in the "Deutsche Nationalbibliografie"; detailed bibliographic data are available on the Internet at http://dnb.d-nb.de/.

Cover design by Nona Reuter

The paper in this book meets the guidelines for permanence and durability of the Committee on Production Guidelines for Book Longevity of the Council of Library Resources.

29 Broadway, 18th floor, New York, NY 10006
www.peterlang.com

Printed in the United States of America

CONTENTS

PREFACE

This book has an unusual and interesting history. It began in the early autumn of 1995 when a Vice Chancellor at my College, N. Brent Kennedy, invited me to represent our institution at an international university fair to be held in Istanbul, Turkey. Dr. Kennedy had drawn a connection between Turkey and the southeastern United States in his book, *The Melungeons: The Resurrection of a Proud People* (Atlanta: Mercer University Press, 1995), which argued that a mysterious subculture in America (the Melungeons) were actually descendants of Ottoman Turks. This research of Brent Kennedy's had fostered a relationship between our region (the Appalachian Mountains of Southwestern Virginia), where many Melungeons had settled, and the Turkish Republic. My trip to Turkey, with College Provost George Culbertson, was to extend that connection through exchange agreements with various universities in Turkey (especially The University of Istanbul) and our academy, The University of Virginia's College at Wise.

While Dr. Culbertson and I met with various Turkish officials, academic, governmental, cultural, and business, I noticed the ubiquitous portrait of Kemal Atatürk in almost every office we visited. As I made inquiries into this founder of Modern Turkey and his political principles, I began to notice similarities between his ideas and many in an American Founder, Thomas Jefferson. As a scholar of Early American political philosophy, I detected an uncanny resemblance between the ideals of republicanism, freedom of religion, liberty of conscience, public education, economic development, and national independence found in Atatürk and Jefferson. I mentioned this to several of our hosts, especially our able guide and translator, Mehmet Topcak. This aroused the Turks' interest.

About six months after returning from my first trip to Istanbul, Vice Chancellor Kennedy called me to say that the Turkish government was intrigued by my remarks on the similarity of Jefferson and Atatürk and would support my research in that area with another trip to Istanbul and Ankara. In the spring of 1997, I visited numerous university libraries, institutes, academics, and government and religious officials in Turkey, gathering information for this book. Too many persons to mention were exceedingly kind in providing books, articles, references, and personal reflections that informed this work. My twenty-year study and writing on Jefferson's political thought (especially my books *The Political Philosophy of Thomas Jefferson*, Johns Hopkins University Press, 1991, and *What Would Jefferson Say*? Penguin, 1998) informed this current study, as did Lord Patrick Kinross's outstanding biography of Kemal Atatürk.

This book will be published worldwide, in the English and Turkish languages, and my hope is that it will show similarities in political theory in Turkey and the United States, between the West and the East, that will bring the world's peoples closer together. If it teaches people of different cultures greater similarities, affection, and understanding, it will have accomplished its purpose.

Soli Deo Gloria.

Garrett Ward Sheldon
Autumn, 1999

INTRODUCTION

At first glance, Thomas Jefferson and Kemal Atatürk seem to be unusual compatriots. Jefferson, the eighteenth-century North American philosopher and a Founder of the United States; and Atatürk, the twentieth-century soldier of the Ottoman Empire and Founder of the modern Republic of Turkey, seem separated by history, culture, and temperament. Yet a closer examination of these two historic political figures reveals striking similarities in background, interests, and ideals. From their growing up in vast, but decaying, empires to their leading national independence movements, to their shared ideals of representative democracy, economic equality and progress, religious freedom and liberty, and love of the countryside, Thomas Jefferson (the icon of American civilization) and Kemal Atatürk (the hero of Modern Turkey) show remarkable kinship across cultural and historical landscapes. This book examines these common characteristics and ideals in Jefferson and Atatürk, showing that distance and culture are not barriers to shared sacred ideals and practices. Although many specific differences exist between these two leaders, the extent of similarity, given their contrasting environments and times, is an encouragement to all who believe in the commonality of humanity, wherever and whenever found on the globe.

Thomas Jefferson was raised a loyal British subject of the vast British Empire; Kemal Atatürk grew up as a loyal subject of the great Ottoman Empire. Both led the revolutions that toppled those venerable Imperial realms, and each created a new, vital republic in their place. Both appealed patriotically to the "best" of their nations' past: Jefferson, the Ancient English Constitution of individual rights and participatory democracy; Atatürk, the honor and destiny of the Turkish people. Each derided the decadent, corrupt state of the old regime: Jefferson, the opulent and oppressive British Parliament and Crown; Atatürk, the weak and ineffective Sultanate and Caliphate.

Finally, for both Jefferson and Atatürk, the agonizing separation from the past had to occur and each became a leader in the Revolutionary Wars of Independence in their countries. Both displayed a breadth of knowledge and dedication to national independence that attracted others who recognized Jefferson and Atatürk as natural leaders. Each seemed to know the pulse of the common people, their values and aspirations, so that others followed them easily. Jefferson and Atatürk's contemporaries admired their forceful dedication to their nation's cause, their fearless devotion to their countries welfare and independence. Jefferson, the philosopher, used his pen more than the sword, and Atatürk, the soldier, used the sword more than the pen; but both organized the national resistance to Imperial oppression effectively through intelligence and their magnetic personalities. Both insisted that the battle for national independence was not for a restoration of the past but for an entirely new political system in America and Turkey: a democratic republic. Each authored a "Declaration of Independence" extolling principles of republican government by the consent of the people. Both became outlaws to the old Empires.

After the revolutionary Wars of Independence, both Jefferson and Atatürk enunciated principles of self-government. Jefferson's pyramid of republics, from ward to state to nation; Atatürk's Constitution of popular sovereignty, parliamentary elections and rotation of office were very radical governments for the time and setting in America and Turkey. Each ushered in the modern form of society and politics in their respective countries.

A key component of a modern republic, for Jefferson and Atatürk, was freedom of religion. Each had grown up in a society with a state religion: The official Church of England for Jefferson and the official Islamic state for Atatürk. Both saw the legal involvement of religion in politics as corrupting both religion and politics. Both were accused of being anti-religious but in reality Atatürk and Jefferson held deep religious faiths. In fact, their appeals for individual liberty of religious conscience was for the true faith to come about. Only uncoerced, freely-chosen religious belief was pleasing to God, so all restrictions on hearing different religions must by removed. Absolute liberty of belief, expression, and evangelism must be respected in a democratic, modern republic. In both America and Turkey religious freedom, including the right of adults to change their beliefs or religious faith, has increased religion and morality in their respective countries. Tolerance for minority faiths and individual freedom of belief foster vital religion and aid societal ethics. Each leader saw freedom of religion as essential to a progressive and moral society.

Likewise, both Jefferson and Atatürk saw education as essential to self-government. Each inherited a society in which education was only for the privileged few; and each helped establish a public education system that elevated the average citizen to literacy and intelligence. Both knew that equality of opportunity required equality of basic education and that the entire country would benefit from a generally educated populace.

Jefferson and Atatürk also saw the integral place of economics to democratic society and the need for a mix of private enterprise and government regulation of business. Each understood the potential for authoritarian concentration of wealth and corruption of the government if property was not widely distributed and taxes fairly appropriated. A balance of innovative capitalist freedom and public regulation of the economy for the common good is found in both Atatürk and Jefferson. Each was particularly drawn to the native countryside and the need for a strong agricultural base for the economy.

The legacies of Jefferson and Atatürk remain unique in their respective countries, the United States of America and The Republic of Turkey. Scholars have noted that America sees itself through its image of Thomas Jefferson; he is the "archetypical American": lover of individual liberty; inventive in technology; believer in the common citizen; patriot of the nation. Similarly Atatürk more than any other person, represents Turkey to its people; his courage, honesty, determination, strength, and dedication to country is the model for modern Turks. Both Jefferson and Atatürk represent their nations abroad; the world recognizes Jefferson as the "author" of American independence and Atatürk as the Founder of Modern Turkey. Each is a prominent figure in the modern world.

This book examines in detail these similarities between Thomas Jefferson and Kemal Atatürk. It shows that what appear on the surface very different personalities, cultures, and historical periods actually share many fundamental similarities and ideals.

CHAPTER ONE

THE IMPERIAL SETTING

Jefferson

The part of the eighteenth-century British Empire in North America that became the United States was settled by English, Scots, Irish, Dutch, and German peoples for a variety of reasons (economic, religious, political, and personal). This British Imperial context affected Thomas Jefferson's view of politics just as the Ottoman Empire greatly affected Kemal Atatürk's view of politics and society. Both Jefferson and Atatürk grew up in large empires; both led revolutions to transform those empires (or portions of them) into new nations; both Jefferson and Atatürk rejected many aspects of the imperial societies that raised them.

The great Historian of the British North American Colonies, Samuel Eliot Morison in *The Oxford History of the American People*, points out that the region that became the U.S.A. began as an integral portion of the vast British Empire (just as present-day Turkey was part of the vast Ottoman Empire) but was always fairly independent from the Mother country because of the distance from the Crown and Parliament in London.[1] The American colonies in the eighteenth century were ruled by the King of England and Parliament, shared British laws, culture, religion, and history with the British Isles and regarded the Mother Country with respect and affection (235). Yet these British dominions enjoyed special privileges that subjects in the home country lacked. Self-government was practiced in the colonial assemblies; land ownership was largely free of feudal tenure restrictions; churches in many areas (especially New England) were free from the Established Anglican Church; maximum wages were not fixed by law; Americans were exempt from compulsory naval service; freedom of conscience, speech and press were enjoyed, occupations were open to the talented rather than restricted by Trade Guilds; taxes were minimal and laws were light (235–236). The central British Imperial state practiced a kind of "benign neglect" over the North American Colonies. Until the Seven Years' War (1756–1763) between Britain (and her Colonists) and France (and her Native American Indian allies) the Empire felt little obligation or need of the North American Colonies. After this war, which ended France's presence in North America, except for Quebec, Canada, Great Britain had accumulated a large war debt incurred battling French Canada and Spanish Florida (247). It seemed only fair to the British Sovereign, King George III, that the North American Colonies contribute to the paying off of this war debt that protected their independence and rights as Englishmen and continue to contribute to the British defense of those regions (247). Hence the Crown and Parliament imposed new taxes on the Americans beginning with the Revenue Act of 1764 and the Stamp Act of 1765. These led, eventually, to the American War of Independence and the creation of a new nation, the United States of America. The tax amounts were fairly insignificant, but they represented an assertion of a "foreign" power and domination that eventually led to a breach, just as the peace accords ending World War I and carving up the Ottoman Empire imposed a foreign oppression on Turkey, causing the remnant of the Turks, led by Atatürk, to fight their war of independence.

From the American Colonists' view, the British justification for the new Imperial taxes was illegitimate, as most of the fighting on the North American continent during the Seven Years' War was conducted by the Colonists (with little aid from the British army or navy and with little expense to the Empire) (234). It seemed to the Colonists that the Empire was exploiting them to support the King's wars in Europe. This perception caused the Colonists to resist these new taxes, which in turn caused the Empire to assert its power more over North America, imposing new laws, political practices, economic regulations, and religious requirements on the American subjects. This new assertion of British cultural domination on the Colonists led to the fiercest resistance to the British Realm, culminating in American Independence. The traditional imperial practice of colonial governor's instruction coming from the king was more rigorously enforced, increasing friction with colonial legislatures. Trials in Admiralty Courts (without benefit of local juries) antagonized the colonists, as did Royal appointment and tenure of judges (243). In 1763, the British Archbishop of Canterbury, head of the official state church, proposed establishing bishops in the North American colonies, imposing the legal religion with its liturgy and theology on the colonists, many of whom were dissenters (Presbyterian, Congregationalist, Baptist, Quakers). This alarmed many of the Christians in North America, who had emigrated precisely to practice religious liberty (244). Many Historians attribute the American Revolution and national independence to this religious concern and deeply held belief in freedom of conscience and faith. Certainly the fervor of resistance to British domination is best explained not by economic or political motives but by liberty of conscience in matters relating to God (244).

However, the concerns over the enforcement of these new British taxes fueled resistance in America. The use of general search warrants to catch smugglers and tax evaders angered the Colonists because unlimited police searches of private citizens' houses violated a sacred right of the Englishman to domestic peace and tranquility. A lawyer defending a client against such a general search warrant claimed the privilege of privacy in one's home as "natural law"—part of "the unchangeable unwritten code of Heaven" (249).

Britain further antagonized the American people by issuing a Royal order in 1763 forbidding westward expansion on the continent. The King hoped to populate the eastern seaboard by this policy, but it frustrated American farmers' use of new lands and land investors' profits, including George Washington (249).

The new taxes were fairly minor: the Revenue Act levied duties on foreign sugar and luxury goods (wine, silk, etc.) imported into America; the Stamp Act required a legal stamp or permit be affixed on paper documents (deeds, diplomas, newspapers, ads, wills, etc.). The rates were low, but the inconvenience and sense of oppression was high (250–251). Resistance to the taxes was so great that the British Parliament repealed the Stamp Act of 1766. However, His Majesty's Government at the same time reaffirmed its right to tax Americans and to rule them "in all cases whatsoever" (254). The Royal government yielded under colonial pressure, but it hardened its attitude and increased its potential domination.

The Townshend Act of 1767 restored British taxation on the North American colonies. It imposed taxes on English goods imported to America such as tea, paper, cloth, glass, and paint (257). Again, the American colonists saw this as an unconstitutional imposition on their rights to govern their own political and economic affairs and the entering wedge of British domination over their whole social organization (260–261). Resistance to these taxes ultimately led directly to the American War of Independence. Beginning with colonial boycotts of taxed British imports and consumption of native tea, liquor, and homespun cloth, eventually the resistance to Imperial regulation of commerce exploded into the destruction of British property and violent confrontation. Ironically, it was the British imported tea from India, re-exported to North America that tipped the Colonies toward Revolution. Resistance to the Townshend Act caused the Crown and Parliament to repeal all the duties on British goods except tea. This one item, however, was retained to symbolize British domination over America (269). As Lord Chatham said of the Colonists at the time: "They must be subordinate. In all laws relating to trade and navigation especially, this must be the mother country, they are the children; they must obey, and we must prescribe" (270). Such haughty British parents soon found that this arrogant way of ruling their American children, just like their later imperious treatment of the defeated Turks after World War I, led to resistance and rebellion. Jefferson's early writings also evince a profound anguish over separating from the British Empire. This separation from the affectionate ties to America's mother country was a kind of death to him, revealing the familial ties engendered by the original English settlement.[2] The Empire was a Family. In his *Summary View of the Rights of British America* (1774), Jefferson beseeched the king to restore "fraternal love and harmony thro' the whole empire," securing a "well-poised empire" of harmony and reciprocity.[3] And even more in his revolutionary tract, *The Declaration of the Causes and Necessity for Taking up Arms* (1775), Jefferson attributes the colonies' prior toleration of Parliament's incursions into their affairs to the "warmth of affection" between America and "Mother England" (199). The separation, like divorce, was painful. Jefferson wrote to John Randolph of the "unnatural contest" ensuing between the colonies and Britain, to which he was "looking with fondness towards a reconciliation" (241). He hoped unity would be restored.

When those affectionate ties to Britain were stretched beyond endurance, Jefferson felt forced to sever allegiance with the realm, despite his personal anguish. This only occurred when the Crown made war on the colonies, when Britain chose to enforce its dictates not merely with the established forms of rule or even indigenous English soldiers, but with "Scotch and foreign mercenaries."[4] This, for Jefferson, was a kind of treason, and it provided "the last stab to agonizing affection," bidding him to "renounce forever these unfeeling brethren" and to advise his fellows to "forget our former love for them" (427).

Jefferson's emotional and at times conflicting sentiments over American separation from Britain derived in part from the prevailing imperial ideology and the changes that had occurred in the British Empire since the original settlements under Elizabeth I. The English colonies in America had originally been settled in the seventeenth-century under a benign feudal monarch and were governed by an ideology and within a structure appropriate to royal dominions. That ideology conceived of a realm that integrated politics, economics, society, and religion into an organic whole ruled by a single sovereign under God's natural law, not unlike the Ottoman Empire. This vision of a traditional organic realm was simply extended to the vast British Empire, including colonies within an integral dependency premised in royal allegiance and feudal land tenure. Diversity could exist within the whole. Sir Francis Drake conducted his naval adventures and acquired colonial possessions in the name of his queen; Charles I proclaimed Virginia to be a part of the royal empire.

Originally, the formal political structure of the American colonies represented this monarchical order. The Crown's control over colonial politics was ubiquitous. Legitimate territorial existence was granted by royal charters; ruling colonial officials (governor and council) were appointed by the Crown; laws enacted by inferior public assemblies were sent back to London for the king's approval and then returned as royal decrees, showing their dependence on Britain. The actual gravitation of political authority to the popular colonial assemblies did nothing to alter this technical imperial structure. Of course, the distant American colonies soon became much more self-reliant and independent.

This position that the American colonists found themselves in, as distant members of an organic, traditional realm, accounted for their feelings of both affection for, and resentment of, the royal British Empire. To complicate matters further, the English themselves were increasingly uncomfortable with that traditional monarchical ideology, and after the Glorious Revolution of 1688 and the establishment of parliamentary supremacy, the royal and feudal ideology was retained only as a kind of vague romantic fiction, which caused an equally dramatic change in imperial relations. For, as sovereignty in England shifted from the Crown to Parliament, the British Empire became increasingly commercial, as the merchant class became more influential in Parliament. As mercantilist interests grew, the former conduct of the old empire diminished: in place of expansion for the honor, religion, and virtue of the royal sovereign and his realm, the empire grew for purely commercial purposes; in place of integral dependencies within the royal "family" of states, the colonies became objects of purely economic and military concern; more like pawns than partners. Yet, while Parliament and its commercial interests assumed control of the empire, they tried to retain the benign organic royal ideology which had originally established it.[5] This infusion of British military and commercial conduct in the guise of traditional ideology contributed to the American colonists' confusion and resentment, and fueled their desire for national independence.[6]

This desire for freedom was given means of expression by the very ideas that English parliamentarians used to topple the monarchy. The Ancient Constitution and liberal natural rights philosophy, used so effectively by the seventeenth-century English in their ideological battles with the Crown, came back to haunt them one hundred years later when the American colonists used the same approach to destroy the last vestige of royal supremacy: the traditional ideology of the royal British empire. Theories of a virtuous Ancient Constitution and inherent natural rights could not be enshrined in native British politics and law by Parliamentarians without eventually finding their way to the growing class of colonial lawyers.[7] Armed with these theories, the American revolutionaries faced an imperial ideology which strangely mixed royal sovereignty based in feudal land tenure and parliamentary supremacy pursuing mercantilist policies. Thomas Jefferson became the exemplary revolutionary theorist as he skillfully invoked the leading philosophical arguments for American independence, using ideas familiar to his British imperial opponents.

He drew upon two common theoretical justifications for American independence: (1) the Ancient Constitution, whose venerable Saxon liberties provided historical precedent for colonial rights; (2) Lockean liberalism, whose abstract principles of natural right legitimated colonial claims through nature itself. To both of these arguments for American independence, Jefferson brought an unusual breadth and depth of knowledge, acquired from studies extending through the classics in both law and history. His understanding of the Ancient Constitution was not limited to the common writers of that myth, but included the entire common law tradition of English jurisprudence; his debt to the liberal heritage of John Locke is not only evident, but extraordinarily clear, distinct and learned. Jefferson's use of the Ancient Constitution and Lockean natural rights philosophy must be understood in their context—both were used to support the arguments of revolutionary colonies wishing independence from a traditional empire which had been corrupted with parliamentary mercantilism and autocratic government. However, even when Jefferson attacked the corruption of parliamentary politics and commercialism, he did not invoke the classical republican language of virtue, but the rights of the Ancient Constitution. In the process of transplanting these venerable truths to American shores, he formulated an original, federated conception of the British Empire. Just as Atatürk later accused the Sultan of corrupting the strength of the Ottoman Empire, Jefferson saw George III weakening the British Empire.

In England, the "Ancient Constitution" consisted of that "perfect liberty" embodied in the principles and practices of government during the prefeudal Saxon tribes prior to the Norman invasion.[8] It was seen as a "golden age" of English liberty, free from the decadent influences of monarchical authority and feudal tenure. This Ancient Constitution supposedly secured the freedom of individuals to participate in making governmental policies affecting their private property (notably taxation) and the freedom from governmental regulation of their private conduct in economic, political, social, and religious matters.[9] The principles of this venerable constitution were extremely hostile to monarchical feudalism, which regarded all landed property within the realm as possessed and granted by the sovereign—that is, it was inherently republican.

The Ancient Constitution's view of human nature (as free and independent individuals) and politics (as a limited, consensual state) bore a striking resemblance to the Lockean liberal view of man and society, with one notable exception: these ideas, by deriving from an *ancient* source, provided historical validity to liberalism by existing *before* the feudal monarchy, which claimed its political legitimacy through tradition and ancestral lineage. It was older than the Kingdom. This notion of a prefeudal Saxon constitution thus served the seventeenth-century parliamentarians, who actually invented it, by providing the substance of modern British liberal doctrine with the advantage of situating their historical claim to liberty in a period antedating the monarchy, whose legitimacy was historical.

Thomas Jefferson learned this concept of the Ancient Constitution from those English jurisprudence scholars who originally developed it. As a loyal British subject studying for the bar after the Glorious Revolution, he could not have avoided imbibing this common doctrine from the law books he was required to read. Furthermore, while Jefferson referred to Sir Edward Coke as "an old dull scoundrel,"[10] his *Commonplace Book* of legal studies reveals ample use of Coke's version of English common law history. In addition, from the archetypical liberal jurisprudence scholar Sir William Blackstone, Jefferson copied a classic description of the "corruption" of ancient Saxon liberties by the Norman conquerors who imposed feudalism on the island: "English liberties are not infringements merely of the king's prerogative, extorted from princes by taking advantage of their weakness; but a restoration of that ancient constitution, of which our ancestors had been defrauded by the art and finesse of the Norman Lawyers, rather than deprived by the force of Norman arms."[11] Jefferson adopted Parliamentary ideas and used them against Parliament.

The principles of the Ancient Constitution found their way into Jefferson's writings directly, as in his passing reference to English history in his *Summary View of the Rights of British America*:

> The introduction of Feudal tenures into the Kingdom of England, though antient, is well enough understood.... In the earlier ages of the Saxon settlement, feudal holdings were certainly altogether unknown.... Our Saxon ancestors held their lands, as they did their personal property, in absolute dominion.... William the Norman first introduced that system generally...but still much was left in the hands of his Saxon subjects...not subject to feudal conditions.[12]

More significantly, these Ancient ideas became transformed by Jefferson's colonial circumstances into a novel theory of empire, a theory leading directly to American independence. Like Atatürk, he used philosophy practically and creatively, for political purposes.

In his *Declaration of the Causes and Necessity for Taking up Arms* (1775), Jefferson gives the English empire one of his many history lessons on the settlement of America, which merges conveniently with the Ancient Constitution: "Our forefathers, inhabitants of the island of Britain, left their native land to seek on these shores a residence for civil & religious freedom. At the expense of their blood, to the ruin of their fortunes...they effected settlements in the inhospitable wilds of America."[13] A year earlier, Jefferson had explained the connection between this American settlement and its Saxon precursor:

> Our ancestors, before their emigration to America, were the free inhabitants of the British dominions in Europe, and possessed a right, which nature has given to all men, of departing from the country in which chance, not choice has placed them...their Saxon ancestors had under this universal law, in like manner, left their native wilds and woods in the North of Europe...and there never was any claim of superiority or dependence asserted over them by that mother country from which they had migrated...no circumstance has occurred to distinguish materially the British from the Saxon migration.[14]

This "universal law" of the "right of departure" which the ancient Saxons exercised is also established in Locke's *Second Treatise*.[15] Elsewhere, Jefferson grounded colonial independence in the "labor" expended acquiring and cultivating the new territory, which also comes directly out of Locke is philosophy.[16]

From Jefferson's rendition of American liberties and de facto independence, following the precedent of their Saxon ancestors, came his new theory of the British Empire. In this theory, the empire was made up of a federation of independent and equal legislatures, colonial (the commonwealths of Virginia, Pennsylvania, and so forth) and domestic (the Parliament in London). These "free and independent" states then chose a common king as an arbiter to protect the rights of each legislature from any threat from foreign nations or each other, i.e., government by consent of the governed. As with the governmental arbiter created by the free and equal individuals out of Locke's state of nature, the British Crown, in Jefferson's view, exercised delegated authority and was strictly limited to protecting the rights of those independent and equal legislatures making up the empire: a social contract government.

As such, Jefferson addressed the King, "his Majesty" as "the chief magistrate of the British empire" and expected him to redress the colonies' "injured rights" from "his imperial throne."[17] He reminded the monarch that a king "is no more than the chief officer of the people," appointed by the people to enhance the "great machine of government" (121). Atatürk, later, said something similar to the Ottoman Sultan. America's participation in the royal empire is not a consequence of the extension of a medieval realm, as much as a blessing bestowed voluntarily by magnanimous colonists on their unfortunate English brethren. As Jefferson explained to George III: "That settlements having been thus effected in the wilds of America, the emigrants thought proper to adopt that system of laws under which they had hitherto lived in the Mother Country, and to continue their union with her by submitting themselves to the same common sovereign, who was thereby made the central link connecting the several parts of the empire thus newly multiplied" (1:122–123). Or, put slightly differently a year later: "To continue their connection with the friends whom they had left they arranged themselves by charters of compact under the same common king, who thus completed their powers of full and perfect legislation and became the link of union between the several parts of the empire."[18] The problem arose, from Jefferson's perspective, when one free and independent legislature within the federated empire (the British Parliament) began legislating for other free and equal legislatures (the colonies) and the supposedly neutral arbiter (the King) collaborated with the usurpers, becoming, in effect, a traitor. The Revenue and Stamp Acts were the most recent examples of this inappropriate tyranny.

So, Jefferson first directed his complaints to Parliament, for exercising sovereign authority beyond its legitimate purview, and second, to the king, for sanctioning and assisting, this usurpation of authority. He declared the imperial compact "invaded by the parliament" in a manner "dangerous to...the British empire"; the idea that "one *free and independent legislature* hereby takes upon itself to suspend the powers of another" (emphasis added) is patently absurd to Jefferson.[19] In the original British Empire, ruled by the absolute authority of a feudal monarch, the dissolution of inferior colonial legislatures would not appear the least bit absurd; but since that monarch had been supplanted by his own inferior legislature in England, Parliament, which now sought to rule the colonies as the king had, it made to Jefferson little sense. Such "unheard of...executive power," wrote Jefferson, constituted a "parliamentary tyranny," to use a Lockean phrase, and justified separation.[20]

While Jefferson concentrated on this formal political corruption of the empire, he also complained of the substantive changes in imperial policy under the increasing parliamentary tyranny. The merchants who controlled Parliament "indulged themselves in every exorbitance which their avarice could dictate."[21] While the Crown had always regulated colonial trade, this Parliament was extending that regulation into area heretofore held sacred. Particularly disturbing to Jefferson and other gentry was the rendering of American lands or estates subject to creditors. This violated the traditional immunity that the landed nobility enjoyed against the "Shylocks" of trade and money-lending (124). It threatened to place gentlemen at the mercy of their social lessers, a fate not welcomed by the heavily indebted Virginia gentry. The inferiority imposed on American gentlemen, like the humiliation of Turkish officers by the Allied Treaty concluding World War I, finally led to revolution.

Having explained to the king of Great Britain "the whole art of government" (134) and the proper ordering of the British Empire, Jefferson now was able to regard George III's contempt for his kind of advice as an abdication of royal authority, effectively eliminating the duty of allegiance owed that sovereign. This must have provided some comfort to Jefferson, for, as he had learned in his legal studies: treason being a breach of allegiance to the king, "if there is no allegiance, there can be no treason."[22] Atatürk later viewed the Sultan's collaboration with the Allied invaders exactly the same way. The American colonies' assertion of independence was thus presented not as a breaking of legitimate ties to a traditional realm, but the reclaiming of their original ancient liberties from an irresponsible and corrupt monarchy, just as Atatürk concluded that serving a corrupt Sultan who sold his realm to the enemy was treasonous. Both Jefferson and Atatürk put patriotism to country above loyalty to a sovereign.

Unfortunately, those theories of Jefferson's which relied on the mythical Ancient Constitution also suffered historical inaccuracies, which eventually undermined the intellectual consistency of some of his revolutionary arguments. For, if the liberal jurisprudence scholars from whom Jefferson borrowed erroneously premised their assaults on the monarchy in the nonexistent liberties of a mythical Ancient Constitution, Jefferson's imperial theories beholden to those scholars would share the taint of their mistakes. In both cases, the major historical blind spot would be the *feudal* basis of social organization and the common law tradition. Sir Edward Coke, as Professor Pocock shows, "had no conception that in the early common law he was dealing with the law of a society organized upon feudal principles."[23] As such, it was possible for Coke to simply re-interpret the English common law through strictures adopted from modern natural rights philosophy. However, this reinterpretation could not validate—historically—the pre-Norman Saxon liberties with which the parliamentarian wished to out-precedent the monarchy. For, in fact, the common law tradition did not preserve ancient Saxon liberties which supported parliamentary supremacy; the common law tradition represented the well-developed feudal relations brought to the island by William the Conqueror: "The Common Law was above all a law regulating the tenure of land, and the rules of tenure it contained in fact presupposed the existence of those military and feudal tenures which had been imported by the Normans" (64).

To the extent native Saxons possessed any organized society and government, it was tribal and chieftain rather than the ideal liberal republican order of John Locke. A later critic of the mythical Ancient Constitution described the Saxons as a crowd of "rude, scarce humanized fighting beggars," not free republican citizens.[24]

Jefferson's historical inaccuracies occur most in his interpretation of the settlement of Virginia. In October of 1775, King George III, addressing Parliament on the subject of American colonial unrest, declared that those settlements had been "planted with great tenderness, encouraged with many commercial advantages, and protected and defended at much expense and treasure."[25]

In response to this royal assertion of English nurturance of the American colonies, Jefferson wrote a concise history of Virginia, ostensibly showing the absence of such support and proving the "self-reliance" of American settlers. In his *Refutation of the Argument that the Colonies Were Established at the Expense of the British Nation* (January 1776),[26] Jefferson presented a history of Virginia's settlement, from which any impartial examination would provide ample evidence not only for the king's assertions of British support, but for the feudal origins of that support; yet Jefferson for practical reasons chose to conclude from this same evidence that American colonists were themselves solely responsible for their own settlement; and this historical blindspot may be attributed directly to his adherence to the doctrine of the Ancient Constitution.

For example, he writes that in 1578 Queen Elizabeth granted, by letters of patent to Sir Humphrey Gilbert, a license to search for uninhabited countries, reserving for the Crown of England his allegiance (277). That allegiance effectively transferred his discoveries to the Crown—to then be returned to him legally under the principle of feudal tenure. Elizabeth similarly granted support to Sir Walter Raleigh, with which he declared Newfoundland "in behalf of the Crown of England," afterwards ordaining that the laws of the realm include conformity in religion to the Church of England, and punishment for treason against the Crown (even against disrespectfully speaking of Her Majesty) (278). Raleigh proceeded to parcel out, in the form of feudal vassalage, portions of land to the fishermen by surrounding waters for their use in drying and dressing their fish, in exchange for a yearly rent to him and his heirs (278). In like manner, Raleigh settled Virginia, from which Jefferson concluded that "Raleigh, having received no assistance from the Crown in any of these enterprises and having now expended 40,000 pounds in them, made an assignment to divers gentlemen and merchants of London for continuing the action of inhabiting and planting his people in Virginia." Ironically, for this revolutionary, Jefferson's "Refutation" ends with his observation that subsequent Virginia settlements were sanctioned by King James's 1624 Proclamation.[27]

Later, Jefferson honestly acknowledged "some uncertainties and inaccuracies of historical facts" connected with his appropriation of the Ancient Constitution in his theory of empire and colonial history.[28] However in the heat of revolutionary turmoil, like the chaos after World War I in Turkey, Jefferson refused to admit any errors in his approach, even when confronted with alternative evidence by trusted fellow revolutionaries. Atatürk similarly considered the salvation and independence of his native Turkey more important than ideological purity or theoretical consistency.

For example, in August of 1776, Edmund Pendleton wrote to Jefferson concerning the matter of land distribution in that newly independent state and pointed out the feudal basis of land tenure under the Crown Empire, suggesting that it be retained by the Commonwealth in modified form: "The Charter on which the Colony was founded, intitled every Britain to settle to 50 acres of Land, to be held in Soccage by the Payments of an Annual quitrent.... It upon the whole therefore appears to me best to continue the old mode, transferring rights, former and future quitrents and Escheats to the Common Wealth from the Crown."[29] Jefferson's response to Pendleton's proposal reveals much greater concern over the latter's raising of legitimate feudal tenure as Virginia's base of land ownership than the practical issue of future regulation of land distribution and state revenue.[30] Jefferson said: "The opinion that our lands were allodial possessions [i.e., grants free from feudal tenure obligations] is one which I have very long held, and had in my eye during a pretty considerable part of my law reading which I found always strengthened it" (491).

> But this is only meant with respect to the English law as transplanted here [i.e., the Ancient Constitution]. How far our acts of assembly or acceptance of grants may have converted lands which were allodial into feuds [i.e., from lands independent of royal authority into lands possessed under the crown's feudal tenure] I have never considered. This matter is now a mere speculative point; and we have it in our power to make it what it ought to be for the public good (491).

This rejection of historical truth for revolutionary right and acceptance of an essentially "might makes right" argument is soon followed by Jefferson's general denunciation of the monarchical feudal system, in an attempt to justify his revolutionary position in spite of its obvious tenuousness: "Is not its history well known, and the purposes for which it was introduced, to wit, the establishment of a military system of defense?

Was it not afterwards made an engine of immense oppression? Is it wanting with us for the purpose of military defense? May not its other legal effects…be performed in other more simple ways (492)? Are we not the better for what we have hitherto abolished of the feudal system? Has not every restitution of the antient Saxon laws had happy effects? Is it not better now that we return at once to that happy system of our ancestors, the wisest and most perfect ever yet devised by the wit of man, as it stood before the 8th century (492)?" Me thinks he protests too much.

In a sense, Jefferson was correct in determining the issue of feudal tenure to be irrelevant, though not for the reasons of revolutionary expediency or "antient virtue." Rather, his historical inaccuracies were rendered somewhat irrelevant by their status as errors perpetrated on a fraud—namely the continued existence of the organic (feudal) ideology of the British Empire after Parliament had wrested sovereignty from the monarchy, and the questionable policies of the later Empire.

History had changed the central authority of the British Empire, and it was only fair to acknowledge this fact and make the appropriate structural changes in Imperial relations. Similarly, after the Sultan had lost most of the Ottoman Empire and compromised the center of Turkey with the Allied invaders, Atatürk refused to regard him as the legitimate sovereign any longer.

Atatürk

The Ottoman Empire that Kemal Atatürk was born into in the late nineteenth century was, like the British Empire to Jefferson's America, in decline. From controlling a vast area around the Mediterranean, extending from Vienna to Yemen, Algiers to the Caucasus, the Ottoman Empire had shrunk, in actual power, to an area barely extending beyond the current borders of modern Turkey. Like the British Empire's loss of North America, the Ottoman Empire's loss of power and influence, Atatürk would attribute to corruption and decadence. The "Sick Man of Europe," as the Ottoman Empire came to be known by the nineteenth century was declining, in Atatürk's view, because its government was not serving its own people, but was neglecting and abusing them, and consequently losing its influence.[31] The government administrators of the Ottoman provinces (pashas and hospodas) had come to power by paying large bribes to the central authority and to recover these expenses of acquiring position they taxed and exploited their subjects, reducing the Turkish peasantry to misery and poverty. The same fiscal and political corruption that bred American resistance to the British Empire fueled popular Turkish resistance to the Ottoman Sultans and their Imperial authority. As with the unraveling of the worldwide British Empire, the increasingly corrupt and authoritarian Ottoman Empire lost much of its influence through regional rebellion before foreign domination relieved it of most of its territories. The Arab provinces were in continuous revolt by the early twentieth century and consequently were ungovernable. In the Eastern European provinces, such as Albania, the Ottoman officials were unable to collect taxes or enforce laws. Macedonia was torn by strife between Greeks, Serbs, Bulgarians, and were supported by their Western European and Russian allies in their nationalistic ambitions. To address this disintegration of the Ottoman Empire, various Sultans (like certain British Kings and ministers in the British Empire) instituted some reforms to placate regional interests. Though most of these advances were short-lived or poorly implemented, they paved the way for more substantial reforms in the twentieth century. First in the military, the Ottoman Empire allowed some of its officers to be trained in modern methods by British, Austrian, and Prussian armies, in the mid nineteenth century. Sultan Mahmud II acknowledged the need for education in engineering and medicine for a modern army. Islam came to be more of a unifying element under Sultan Abdulhamid, as the idea of an Ottoman Islamic nation emerged (this, however aggravated the many non-Moslem communities in Turkey and encouraged foreign intervention on their behalf).

In 1838, public primary and secondary schools were established with provisions for teaching French and modern subjects (primarily for government officials and diplomats). Newspapers appeared in Turkey in the 1830s but most were written in French and read by few Turks and carefully censored. In 1834, a national postal system was inaugurated and the requisite postal roads were valuable for connecting different parts of the Ottoman Empire. In 1839, Mahmud II's son Abdulmecid continued his father's reforms with the famous Noble Rescript of the Rose Chamber—a proclamation that guaranteed the Turks rights to life, property, liberty of religion, and fair trial procedures. A legal code affirming Turkish subjects equality before the law was promulgated in 1840. Financial reforms were accomplished by takeovers of foreign capitalists who eroded Ottoman control of its own economy. Turkish railways, mines, and banks increasingly were managed by French and British businesses. Ottoman reliance on foreign capital continued the decline in Turkish society. The fifteen-year reign of Abdulazig beginning in 1861 was characterized by autocratic methods, excessive borrowing of foreign loans, bribes to pashas, the building of new palaces and an extravagant harem (nine hundred women and three thousand eunuchs). Such financial and moral decadence further weakened the Ottoman Empire, paving the way for The Young Turks.

The Young Turks were primarily government and military personnel who had studied in Europe and hoped to save the Ottoman Empire from further decline and self-destruction through democratic reforms and honest, patriotic government. Their ideals were of a Turkey governed by a European-style parliament and modern notions of education, science, economics, and liberal tolerance of national and religious differences within the Empire. Kemal Atatürk, years later, fulfilled the ideals of the Young Turks by leading modern Turkey into parliamentary republic with scientific education, religious freedom, international economics, and technologically advanced military.

Within the context of the Ottoman Empire, the reforms of the Young Turks could not be realized fully. Although in 1908, the central authority of the Young Turk movement, the Committee of Union and Progress, with the support of the Turkish military, proclaimed a constitutional monarchy and freedom of the press was established, the decline and disintegration of the Ottoman Empire continued. Austria-Hungary took advantage of the Turkish disorder and annexed Bosnia and Hercegovina in 1908; King Ferdinand I declared the total independence of Bulgaria and provinces in Albania, and the Arab states agitated against the Turkish Sultan's government.

The Young Turk parliament proceeded to enlist autocratic policies in an attempt to hold onto the Empire, planting Moslem colonies in Macedonia, violence and bribery in elections, repression of political opponents, forbidding free press and assembly, further antagonizing progressives and foreigners alike. Trapped by the corrupt system of the Ottoman Sultans, the reformers, like the liberal ministers of the British Empire, found it impossible to rule without dictatorial methods, which further alienated the Empire's constituencies. This caused disaffected Macedonian provinces to unite against the Empire and seek support from Western Christian countries. In 1911, Italy announced its intention to seize Ottoman possessions in Tripoli and Cyrenaica which led to a war involving Turkish, Arab, and Italian armies. Soon armed uprisings occurred in

Bulgarian, Greek, and Serbian provinces leading to the First and Second Balkan Wars (1912–1913). Meanwhile, Russia encroached upon the Ottoman provinces bordering its territory. The Imperial Turkish government, corrupt and ineffective, was unable to cope with these pressures which culminated in World War I. Allied with Germany, the latter's defeat by Britain and France led to the formal dismemberment of the Ottoman Empire through The Treaty of Sēvres, 1920. Turkey lost Thrace, Cyprus, Egypt Armenia, Mesopotamia, Syria, Palistine, and the islands of Imbors and Tenedos. The Sultan's capitulation to the European destruction of Turkey proved his government's inability to protect or rule its people. It, for Atatürk, like the British Government under King George III for Jefferson, had become a traitor to its own people. Winston Churchill wrote that the Ottoman ruler after World War I, "Loaded with follies, stained with crimes, rotted with misgovernment, shattered by battle, worn down by long disastrous wars, his Empire falling to pieces around him" had become a "puppet Government" (184). Atatürk and the Turkish patriots around him faced a war for the independence of their country from total European dominance with the Ottoman Sultan's willing submission and collaboration. The Turkish War of Independence led by Atatürk would be against the European invaders and the Ottoman government that was siding with them against its own people.

Notes

1. Samuel Eliot Morison, *The Oxford History of the American People*, 3 (N.Y.: Mentor 1972), I:234.
2. Garry Wills inappropriately ascribes Jefferson's sentiments to his intellectual adherence to the Scottish moral sense school (and its doctrine of human sympathy)—see *Inventing America: Jefferson's Declaration of Independence* (New York: Doubleday, 1978), 291. Actually, the sources of Jefferson's anguish are historical and cultural.
3. Thomas Jefferson, *The Papers of Thomas Jefferson*, 20 vols., ed. Julian Boyd (Princeton: Princeton University Press, 1950), 1:135.
4. In Jefferson's Declaration of Independence, 427.
5. J. Holland Rose, A. Newton, and E. A. Benians, eds., *Cambridge History of the British Empire*, (Cambridge: Cambridge University Press, 1929), 207, 214, 614, 622; Klaus E. Knorr, *British Colonial Theories, 1570–1850* (Toronto: University of Toronto Press, 1944); Richard Koebner, *Empire* (Cambridge: Cambridge University Press, 1961), 9–10; David C. Douglass, ed., *English Historical Documents*, 12 vols. (Oxford: Oxford University Press, 1950–1968), 10: 753.
6. See Bernard Bailyn *The Ideological Origins of the American Revolution* (Cambridge: Harvard University Press, 1967). The best attempt to theoretically reconcile this new situation came for Burke's "imperial Parliament"; see his parliamentary speeches in *English Historical Documents*, 10:758–60.
7. Note how many notable revolutionary thinkers were trained as English lawyers. For a good discussion of the role they played in Virginia during the colonial and revolutionary periods, see A. G. Roeber, *Faithful Magistrates and Republican Lawyers* (Chapel Hill: University of North Carolina Press, 1981).
8. J. G. A. Pocock, *The Ancient Constitution and the Feudal Law* (Cambridge: Cambridge University Press, 1957); Bailyn, *Ideological Origins of the American Revolution*, 80–82.
9. Bailyn; Isaac Kramnick, "Republic Revisionism Revisited," *American Historical Review* 87 (June 1982): 638.
10. Jefferson to John Page, December 25, 1762, *Jefferson Papers*, 1: 5.
11. Jefferson, *Commonplace Book*, entry 740.
12. Jefferson, *Jefferson Papers*, 1:132.
13. Thomas Jefferson, *Declaration of the Causes and Necessity for Taking Up Arms*, 1:199.
14. Thomas Jefferson, *A Summary of the Rights of British America*, 1:121–22.
15. John Locke, *The Second Treatise of Government* in *Two Treatises of Government*, ed. Peter Laslett (New York: New American Library, 1965), 8:121–22.
16. Jefferson, *Papers*, 1: 122, 133; and Locke, *The Second Treatise of Government* in *Two Treatises of Government*, ed. Peter Laslett (New York: New American Library, 1965), 5:27, 32–33.
17. Jefferson, *Papers*, 121.
18. Jefferson, *Declaration of Causes and Necessity*, 1:200. See also Jefferson's *Autobiography* (New York: Putnam, n.d.), 31, 40.
19. In Jefferson's draft of the *Declaration of Rights for Virginia* (1774), *Papers*, 1: 119.

20. Jefferson, *A Summary View*, In Jefferson's draft of the *Declaration of Rights for Virginia* (1774), *Papers* 1:126. Compare Locke's comment in the *Second Treatise*, para. 157 and 158: "It often comes to pass that in government where part of the legislative consists of representatives chosen by the people that to tract of time this representation becomes very unequal and disproportionate to the reasons it was at first established. . . .For it being the interest as well as intention of the people to have a fair and equal representative, whoever brings it nearest to that is an undoubted friend to and establisher of the government and cannot miss the consent and approbation of the community" (cited in Kramnick, "Republican Revisionism Revisited," 638).
21. Jefferson, *A Summary View*, 124. J. G. A. Pocock uses this and other colonial references to "corruption" to support his contention that they responded by invoking a "quasirepublican alternative" (*Virtue, Commerce and History* [Cambridge: Cambridge University Press, 1985], 77–83), and that Jefferson called on George III to be Bolingbroke's "Patriot King."
22. Quoted from William Salked's *Reports of Cases in King's Bench* 1689–1712 and copied into Jefferson's *Commonplace Book*, entry 242.
23. The Ancient Constitution, 45.
24. In Kramnick, *Bolingbroke and His Circle*, 130–31.
25. *Parliamentary History*, 18: 696, reprinted in Jefferson, *Papers*, 1: 277.
26. Thomas Jefferson, *Refutation of the Argument that the Colonies Were Established at the Expense of the British Nation, Parliamentary History*, 18: 696, reprinted in Jefferson, *Papers*, 1:277–84.
27. Thomas Jefferson, *Refutation of the Argument that the Colonies Were Established at the Expense of the British Nation, Parliamentary History*, 18: 696, reprinted in Jefferson, *Papers*, 1:278. To George III's assertions premised in that proclamation Jefferson responded that "a King who can adopt falsehood, and solemnize it from the throne, justifies the revolution of fortune which reduces him to a private station."
28. This was in 1809 in reference to Jefferson's *A Summary View, Papers*, 1:670 (appendix).
29. This was in 1809 in reference to Jefferson's *A Summary View, Papers*, 1:484–85. This also shows that Louis Hartz was incorrect in asserting in *The Liberal Tradition in America* (New York: Harcourt Brace, 1955) that America has no feudal past; we had it (albeit in corrupted form) in the organic ideology of the early British Empire.
30. Edmund Pendleton to Thomas Jefferson, August 26, 1776, *Papers*, 1:507.
31. Patrick Kinross, *Atatürk: The Rebirth of a Nation* (London: Weidenfeld, 1964), 15, 23.

CHAPTER TWO
REVOLUTIONARY INDEPENDENCE

Jefferson

The remaining British tax on tea did not simply imply a greater expense on that commodity; it signified for the North American colonists a brutal symbol of Imperial domination that could easily be extended to British political, economic, religious, and social tyranny. The radical "Sons of Liberty" in Boston, like the "Young Turks" that challenged the old Ottoman Empire, tested and provoked this symbol of British domination by a famous act known in history as the Boston Tea Party. One night a group of men, disguised as Mohawk Indians and Africans boarded British ships in Boston Harbor and emptied 342 large chests of English tea into the ocean. This act of defiance caused the British government to retaliate mercilessly. The Boston Port Act of Parliament blockaded that important harbor, economically strangling the region; the Quartering Act imposed British soldiers on the private homes of colonists; and the Quebec Act enshrined French Catholicism in Canada. Together known in America as the Coercive, or Intolerable, Acts, these severe laws pushed the American Colonies into open resistance and rebellion. The Mother Country had become a mean, cruel Father, punishing a disobedient child excessively.

As with the peace accords forced on the Ottoman Empire after World War I, they involved a kind of sadistic humiliation, making it impossible to retain any semblance of self-respect; the American Colonists, as later the Turks, had to resort to armed resistance. Making matters worse, the British government enforced these oppressive laws by altering the Massachusetts government, emphasizing her subservience to Great Britain. The Government and the Administration of Justice Act made the State Council, previously elected by the democratic assembly, appointed by the Royal Governor and, with judges, sheriffs, and justices-of-the-peace, serving only during the King's pleasure. This imposition of monarchical tyranny on Massachusetts prompted the other North American colonies (notably New York, Virginia, and Pennsylvania) to send contributions of food and money to the besieged Community of Boston.[1] Furthermore, the Virginia Assembly called for a day of "fasting and prayer: and issued a resolution declaring that "an attack made on one of our sister colonies, to compel submission to arbitrary taxes, is an attack made on all British America" (277). They proceeded to propose a meeting of a Continental Congress to bring all the colonies together in order to plan resistance to Britain.

Most of the American Colonists still expected a resolution of the crisis within the framework of the Imperial Realm, but continued British domineering, and finally violence, led to revolutionary separation. Attempts were made for reconciliation on both sides, but they failed. In February of 1775, Parliament defeated a bill legalizing the Continental Congress as a governing body in North America, but retaining imperial regulation of trade (280). Had this bill passed, Historian Samuel Eliot Morison believes, no Declaration of Independence or Revolutionary War would have occurred; the North American colonies would never have became the United States of America, but would have remained in Commonwealth status like Canada and Australia (280). However, rather than this reconciling move, the British Government imposed further oppressive measures on New England—in March 1775 forbidding the colonies in that region to trade with any country in the world but Britain and Ireland, as well as denying fishermen use of the shores of Newfoundland and Nova Scotia (281). Benjamin Franklin, negotiating in London at this time, said that if England did not repeal these oppressive measures and remove British soldiers from Boston, even God Almighty could not bring peace (281). Finally an act of violence inflamed the Revolution and American Independence. A British company of soldiers marched to Concord, Massachusetts, to destroy a stash of colonial munitions and met a group of armed colonials at Lexington. The British officer shouted, "Disperse ye rebels, disperse" (285). Someone (it is still not known who) fired a gun, causing both sides to begin shooting, killing eight Americans. This caused the Continental Congress to raise an army, appointing George Washington as Commander. Fighting ensued around the Colonies and a formal Declaration of Independence was proclaimed in July of 1776 (288–296). France assisted the American War against Great Britain and after six years of battles, America received its independence from the British Empire in the Treaty of Paris in February 1783 (350).

Thomas Jefferson played a key role in the ideological battle for American Independence by writing several key Revolutionary pamphlets, including the famous Declaration of Independence. He drew from his studies of British legal philosophy, especially the ideas of John Locke. As I note in my book *The Political Philosophy of Thomas Jefferson*, this adaptation of Lockean ideas served to give a philosophical justification for American statehood.[2]

The best way to show the presence of Locke's political theory in Jefferson's Declaration of Independence is through a thematic treatment of the major theoretical concepts in each text. Three categories represent the major themes of Locke's political philosophy: (1) the nature of man, (2) the nature of government, and (3) the right of revolution. Several striking verbal parallels do exist between Locke's *Second Treatise* and Jefferson's Declaration of Independence, but the substantive thematic parallels are of much greater significance. Simply put, they consist of the following:

1. *The nature of man*: Locke conceives of human nature as involving men who are naturally free, equal, and independent individuals possessed of natural rights, especially that of continued physical existence (life or self-preservation), and of qualities necessarily attending that existence (liberty and property).
2. *The nature of government:* Following from his notion of human nature, Locke's conception of legitimate government consists in that impartial, disinterested arbiter or judge established by those free, equal, and independent individuals possessed of natural rights who by their consent submit to the authority of government constructed to secure their natural rights from the violation of other individuals, or the state.
3. *The right of revolution*: The natural right to abolish established governments follows from the first two Lockean conceptions. Given Locke's definition of human nature and legitimate government, it follows that if the established institutions of government fail to secure the rights they were created to secure (and instead establish a tyranny—invading those rights themselves), it is appropriate for the people to abolish that political structure and erect one that will correctly perform its legitimate function (which is limited to securing individual rights).

Reviewing the relevant portion of Jefferson's Declaration of Independence text in its entirety:

> When in the course of human events it becomes necessary for a people to advance from that subordination in which they have hitherto remained, & to assume among the powers of the earth the equal & independent station to which the laws of nature & of nature's god entitle them, a decent respect to the opinions of mankind requires that they should declare the causes which impel them to change.
>
> We hold these truths to be sacred & undeniable; that all men are created equal & independent, that from that equal creation they derive rights inherent and inalienable, among which are the preservation of life, & liberty, & the pursuit of happiness; and to secure these ends, governments are instituted among men, deriving their just powers from the consent of the governed; that whenever any form of government shall become destructive of these ends, it is the right of the people to alter or to abolish it & to institute new government, laying its foundation on such principles & organizing its powers in such form, as to them shall seem most likely to effect their safety & happiness. Prudence indeed will dictate that governments long established should not be changed for light & transient causes: and accordingly all experience hath shewn that mankind are more disposed to suffer while evils are sufferable than to right themselves by abolishing the forms to which they are accustomed. But when a long train of abuses & usurpations, begun at a distinguished period, & pursued invariably the same object, evinces a design to subject them to arbitrary power, it is their right, it is their duty, to throw off such government & to provide new guards for their future security. Such has been the patient sufferance of these colonies; & such is now the necessity, which constrains them to expunge their former systems of government. The history of his present majesty, is a history of unremitting injuries and usurpation...all of which have in direct object the establishment of an absolute tyranny...let facts be submitted...."[3]

The thematic comparison in the following shows the incontestable theoretical influence of Locke's *Second Treatise* of Jefferson's Declaration of Independence.[4] In Jefferson's Declaration of Independence: "We hold these truths to be scared and undeniable; that all men are created equal and independent." In Locke's *Second Treatise of Government*: "Mankind...being all equal and independent," (ch. 2, 6) "all men by nature are equal," (ch. 4, 54) and "Men being, as has been said, by Nature, all free, equal and independent" (ch. 8, 95). In Jefferson's Declaration of Independence: "from that equal creation they derive rights inherent and inalienable." In Locke's *Second Treatise of Government*: "that equal Right that every man hath, to his Natural Freedom" (ch. 6, 54). In Jefferson's Declaration of Independence: "among which are the preservation of life, and liberty, and the pursuit of happiness." In Locke's *Second Treatise of Government*: "man being born, as has been proved, with a Title to perfect Freedom, and an uncontrolled enjoyment of all the Rights and Privileges of the Law of Nature, equally with any other Man, or number of men in the world, hath by Nature a Power, not only to preserve his Property, that is, his Life, Liberty and Estate, against the Injuries and Attempts of other Men; but to judge of, and punish the braches of that Law in others" (ch. 4, 87), "Everyone as he is bound to preserve himself" (ch. 2, 6), and "Men, being once born, have a right to their preservation" (ch. 5, 25). In Jefferson's Declaration of Independence says, "to secure these ends, governments are instituted...deriving their just powers from the consent of the governed." In Locke's *Second Treatise of Government* says, "Man...seeks...to joyn in society with others...to unite for the mutual Preservation of their Lives, Liberties and Estates" (ch. 9, 123) and "Civil Society is...agreeing with other Men to joyn and unite in a secure Enjoyment of their Properties, and a Greater Security" (ch. 8, 95). In Jefferson's Declaration of Independence says, "to provide new guards for their future security." In Locke's *Second Treatise of Government* says, "And thus that, which begins and actually constitutes any Political Society, is nothing but the consent...of a majority to unite and incorporate into such a society. And this is that, and that only, which did, or could give beginning to lawful Government in the World" (ch. 8, 99), "The Liberty of Man, in Society, is to be under no other Legislative Power, but that established, by consent" (ch. 4, 22), and "Political Power is that Power which every man having in the state of Nature, has given up into the hands of Society, and therein to the Governours.... That is shall be employed for their good, and the preservation of their Property...their Lives, Liberties, and Possessions...only from Compact and Agreement, and the mutual Consent of those who make up the Community" (ch. 15, 171). Again, Jefferson's Declaration of Independence states: "whenever any form of government shall become destructive of these ends, it is the right of the people to alter or abolish it and to institute new government," and "prudence indeed will dictate that governments long established should not be changed for light and transient cause, while Locke's *Second Treatise of Government* states: "When by the Arbitrary Power...without the Consent and contrary to the common Interest of the People, there also the Legislative is altered" (ch. 19, 216), "when the Government is dissolved, the People are at Liberty to provide for themselves, by erecting a new Legislative" (ch. 19, 220), and "Revolutions happen not upon every little mismanagement in public affairs. Great mistakes in the ruling part, many wrong and inconvenient Laws, and all the slips of humans frailty will be born by the people, without mutiny or murmur" (ch. 19, 225). Again, Jefferson's Declaration of Independence states: "mankind are more disposed to suffer while evils are sufferable than to right themselves by abolishing the forms to which they are accustomed," while Locke's *Second Treatise of Government* states: "the People, who are more disposed to suffer, than right themselves by Resistance" (ch. 19, 230). Again, Jefferson's Declaration of Independence states: "but when a long train of abuses and usurpations...pursued invariably the same object, evinces a design to subject them to arbitrary power," while Locke's *Second Treatise of Government* states: "But if a long train of Abuses...all tending the same way, make the design visible to the People" (ch. 19, 225). Again, Jefferson's Declaration of Independence states: "it is their right, it is their duty, to throw off such government to provide new guards for their future security," while Locke's *Second Treatise of Government* states: "'tis not to be wonder'd, that they should then rouze themselves, and endeavor to put the rule into such hands, which may secure to them the ends of which Government was at first erected" (ch. 19, 225).

Now the connection between Locke's ideas and Jefferson's Declaration of Independence is clear; what remains to be shown is the alteration of those liberal ideals by Jefferson's peculiar colonial circumstances, which he accomplished elsewhere in the document.

The "facts submitted" in the Declaration of Independence to prove George III's arbitrary power are less important than that they were addressed to the king. Their content is thus best understood in light of Jefferson's theory of empire; that is, a voluntary federation of "equal and independent" states overseen by an impartial monarch or judge securing the rights of each unity. The primary right to be secured is the fundamental condition of political existence: local, autonomous control of legislation. It is this essential right of democratic sovereignty that these enumerated complaints entail:

1. The king "has refused his assent to laws the most wholesome and necessary for the public good;"
2. "he has forbidden his governors to pass laws;"
3. "he has refused to pass other laws unless those people would relinquish the right of representation";
4. "he has dissolved Representative house;"
5. "he has refused...others to be elected;"
6. he has prevented immigration to colonies and new land appropriations;
7. he has refused to assent to laws establishing judiciary powers;
8. he has made judges dependent on his will;
9. he has erected multitudinous new offices;
10. he has kept standing armies in times of peace;

11. he has rendered the military above the civilian authority;
12. he has subjected us to "a jurisdiction foreign to our constitutions" (e.g., Parliament);
13. he has protected usurpers with mock trials;
14. he has cut off colonial trade with the world;
15. he has "imposed taxes on us without our consent;"
16. he has deprived us of "trial by jury;"
17. he has transported defendants across the sea;
18. he is "taking away our charters & altering fundamentally the forms of our governments;"
19. by "suspending our own legislature."

As such, King George III, for Jefferson, had violated the rights of the American colonies, and thereby abdicated his government "declaring us out of his allegiance & protection."[5] This allowed the colonies to "reject and renounce all allegiance & subjection to the kings of Great Britain...and declare these colonies to be free and independent states" just as Atatürk declared Turkish independence from the Ottoman Sultan and provinces that collaborated with the Allied conquerors (427).

So, Jefferson adapted the language of Lockean liberalism, created originally by Locke for individual men in the state of nature, to the needs of revolutionary colonies or political units in a federated empire of supposed equal and independent states. He therefore refers to "a people['s]" necessity to assume "equal and independent" status, meaning American legislatures attaining proper equality with the British legislature.[6] Locke's "free and independent" individuals are translated into Jefferson's "free and independent states," revealing the distinctive adaptation of Locke's theories to the needs of revolutionary colonies, and tying his ideas to Parliamentary progenitors.[7]

As with Atatürk during the Turkish war of independence, Jefferson uses Modern liberal, republican philosophies to establish a new nation, and abolish the old, corrupt empire.

Atatürk

The Turkish struggle for national independence after World War I transformed Kemal Atatürk from purely a military character into a soldier—politician—statesman who maneuvered the old, declining Ottoman Empire into the modern republican nation of Turkey. Like Jefferson, Atatürk earned the admiration of his compatriots for his breadth and diversity of skills. As his biographer Lord Kinross noted, "only Kemal had the necessary over-all grasp both of internal and external affairs, that peculiar compound of intuition and reason, resilience and energy and above all will-power, required to carry such a hazardous enterprise to a successful conclusion."[8] Atatürk inspired others towards national independence by combining the military skill of a George Washington, the diplomatic statesmanship of a Benjamin Franklin, and the political philosophy of Thomas Jefferson. Like the American Revolutionaries, he saw the struggle for Turkish independence and abandonment of the Ottoman monarchy as *preserving* the true Turkish state. His was, in Lord Kinross's works, "the ambition of a patriot, bound up with what he saw to be his country's interests" (164). Like Jefferson (who was a "backwoodsman" in Albemarle County of Piedmont, Virginia, compared to the old Dominion aristocracy of the Tidewater region), Atatürk was of middle-class background compared to his established, aristocratic colleagues Rauf, Fuad, and Refet; but like the young Jefferson, he led those "gentleman" with his keen intellect and fierce dedication, while being able better than the nobility to relate to the common people in Turkey (164). He identified with the Turkish farmer and laborer, their pride in their heritage and love of the land. Like those average Turkish subjects, Kemal felt a sense of shame and dishonor over the decline of his country—its exploitation by decadent rulers and foreign oppressor. Like Jefferson's Revolutionary appeal to the Ancient Constitution of his Saxon forbearers, Kemal saw the true, simple rural Turk as the core of his civilization robbed by effete Sultans and to be regained by a republic of the simple, average Turkish citizen (165). Like Jefferson's agarian values of a sturdy yeoman class of democratic farmer—citizens, Atatürk looked to the traditional heartland for the future of his country (165).

And just as the British occupation of the North American colonies, and the employment of foreign (Hessian) mercenaries to dominate the country, fueled a nationalist zeal, the Allied occupation of Smyrna roused the popular Turkish spirit of resistance to foreign domination and urged a sentiment of national independence (164–166).

In his capacity as a regional military inspector after the Armistice, Atatürk sent repeated angry telegrams to the War Ministry in Istanbul about the British encroachments on Turkish territory (their reinforcement of troops in the interior, their arming of Greek partisans, their movement into new areas against the terms of the Armistice), causing the central government to recall him (166). Atatürk refused to return and instead moved his operations to the Hauza region which was a center of republican resistance to the foreign dominated Ottoman government. He called local Resistance leaders together and told them of the invaders, "They do not seek to kill us. They seek to bury us alive in our graves. Now we are on the edge of the pit. But if we stir ourselves to a final effort, we may still be saved" (167). Like Patrick Henry's "Give me liberty or give me death," Kemal asserted a national independence from the slavery of safe but humiliating domination. Like Jefferson's *Notes on the State of Virginia*, which formulated the economic and cultural basis of America independence, Atatürk gathered vast information on internal Turkey as a basis for a national revolutionary war and future nationhood (168).

A number of Defense of Rights Associations was emerging around Turkey, which like the American colonial Committees of Safety, formed the nascent governing structures of the new national government. Until independence was secured, these Defense of Rights groups formed the organizations through which Atatürk led the revolution.

The Turkish nationalists led by Kemal, wrote a "Declaration of Independence" which argued that their country was now occupied by foreign powers and the Ottoman capital was controlled by these forces hostile to the Turkish nation. Resistance to this usurpation of national authority required an alternative government through a new Congress faithful to the Turkish people's interests (171). The first two provisions read: (1) The Independence of the nation and the unity of the country are in danger, (2) The Istanbul Government is not performing the requirements for the responsibilities they have undertaken. This situation is showing that our country has virtually ceased to exist."[9] Like the American Continental Congress, which replaced the rule of British Governors and Councils in the North American colonies, the Sivas Congress began modern Turkish nationhood (171).

This Declaration of Independence was cabled to Turkish army units and Defense of rights groups around the country, just as the American Declaration of Independence was communicated throughout the colonies by Committees of Correspondence (172–173). Just as the American revolutionaries' actions caused the British government to attempt to suppress these alternative colonial governments, the Turkish resistance led the Ottoman Minister of the Interior to issue a command that no government or military personnel correspond with Kemal (172). Atatürk was pronounced a "dangerous man, a mutineer, a traitor" and the imminent Congress an illegal assembly (172).

Atatürk resigned his commission as an officer of the Turkish army but declared that henceforth he would fight as an individual "for the achievement of our sacred national purpose" (177). He was immediately elected Chairman of the Erzurum Defense of Rights Association and led plans for the Congress. The Erzurum Congress met in July 1919 and elected Atatürk its first president. At the initial meeting, Kemal gave an address that established the ideological foundations of the new Turkish government. Its two leading principles were (1) the rights of the nation and (2) the will of the people (179). He spoke of the "dark and tragic dangers" that surrounded their country, but also of "the undaunted spirit that inspires the national movement and which, like an electric flash, penetrates even to the remotest parts of our country" (179). The legitimate goal of the revolution for independence was a Turkey which could control its national destiny, deriving its governmental authority from the will of the majority (179). This message, representing an ideal of Western republican government, was reiterated by the independence movement across Anatolia. Like Jefferson's Declaration of Independence, this unified national will.

The Congress's principle document was The Nation pact, which proclaimed the necessity for the preservation of existing Turkish borders and Turkish self-determination guaranteed by an elected provisional government. The Ottoman Government responded, like the British towards the American Revolutionaries, by issuing a warrant for Kemal's arrest.

Atatürk replied by telling the Grand Vizier in a telegram that his Cabinet in Istanbul was one of "complete incompetence" incapable of leading the nation "in its struggle for life and independence" (182). The old regime, Atatürk insisted, must convene a new Parliament to represent the national will and well-being (183).

A Sivas Congress opened in September of 1919 with only a quarter of the nation's population represented but the core of the heartland committed (186). Atatürk was again elected Chairman. This body reaffirmed the National Pact for Turkish Independence and enlisted more army units in its support. Like the early Continental Congresses, it was careful not to attack the Sultan directly, but only the corrupt Cabinet and puppets of the Allied invaders (193). Its General Assembly, however, declared itself the provisional Government of Turkey. This Government gained such power that it forced the Sultan to dismiss the Grand Vizier and formed a new Parliament (196). The British dissolution of that Parliament and occupation of Constantinople, however, forced the revolutionaries to reconvene a Grand National Assembly in Ankara in April 1920, which elected Atatürk president and drafted a constitution and established the new Turkish Republic (208–211, 218–222).

In March 1921, The Turkish Grand National Assembly accepted a new national anthem; its last two lines expressed the dream of an independent Turkey:

> "My flag that lived freely has the right to freedom;
> My nation who worships God,
> Has the right to independence" (69)!

In the same year, Atatürk wrote of himself: "Freedom and independence are in my character. I am a man who was created with a love of independence...for honor, self-respect, integrity and humanity to take root and live in a nation it is absolutely dependent on that nation possessing freedom and independence...national independence is a matter of life and death" (76).

Atatürk belief in national independence is reflected in a famous speech to the young people of Turkey, made on October 20, 1927, and repeated to Turkish youths ever since:

> "Oh Turkish youth! Your first duty is to protect and defend forever the Turkish Independence and the Turkish Republic.... The sole principle of existence and the future is this. This principle is your most valuable treasure...there will be internal and external enemies who will want to deprive you of this treasure...defend Independence and the Republic...O Turkish child of future generations! ...it is your duty to save the Turkish Independence and the Republic" (146).

Kemal Atatürk was aware of the difficulties and tragedies of the War of Independence, but as he wrote to a journalist friend, "In spite of everything, we are certainly walking towards a brilliant light" (146).

Notes

1. Morison, *The Oxford History of the American People,* I: 277.
2. Garrett Ward Sheldon, *The Political Philosophy of Thomas Jefferson* (Baltimore: Johns Hopkins University Press, 1996), 42–51.
3. This is Jefferson's "Original Rough Draught," i.e., his fair copy as prepared for the Committee and prior to Congress's revisions, in *Papers*, 1: 423–27.
4. See Garrett W. Sheldon, *The Political Philosophy of Thomas Jefferson*, 42–51. The phrases of John Locke's are extracted from the best edition available of his *Second Treatise of Government*, in *Two Treatise of Government*, ed. Peter Laslett (New York: New American Library, 1965).
5. Jefferson, *Papers*, 1: 425. The remaining complaints concern Britain's resorting to violence to impose its will on America. Reference is made to the real or threatened use of foreign mercenaries, "Indian savages," American loyalists, and insurgent slaves for this purpose, 425–26.
6. Or, as Jefferson writes elsewhere, "these colonies," *Papers*, 424.
7. *Papers*, 427. Further evidence for this view of Jefferson's adaption of Lockean principles to revolutionary purposes appears in an early letter referring to the "independent rights" of "our...country"; see Jefferson to Archibald Cary and Benjamin Harrison, December 9, 1774, *Papers*, 154.
8. Kinros, *Atatürk*, 164.
9. Mehmet Ozel, *Atatürk* (Ankara: Ajans – Turk Publ., 1991), 53.

CHAPTER THREE

THE REPUBLIC

Jefferson

After winning the Revolutionary War of Independence, the British Colonies of North America established a republic through The United States Constitution (see Appendix A). A Federal Convention in the city of Philadelphia wrote this relatively brief document which set out the structure of the national government, terms, and conditions of office, powers of the various branches of federal government, and its relation to the remaining state regimes.[1] The American Constitution now that oldest founding document in the world, established a state characterized by "federalism" or "two-tier" government: (1) national for foreign and common concerns and (2) state or regional governments for local or domestic concerns. This Constitutional federalism, written in 1787 and ratified by the States in 1789, created The United States of America. During this time, Thomas Jefferson was American Minister to France, so he was involved in the drafting and passing of the U.S. Constitution only indirectly (primarily by correspondence with his friend and fellow Virginian, James Madison, "The Father of the Constitution"),[2] but his later interpretation of that system of government greatly affected American politics for many years. Because the United States Constitution sets up two tiers of government (centralized national in Washington, D.C., and decentralized state in Virginia, New York, Massachusetts, Connecticut, and so forth), the boundaries of their respective authorities are always open to dispute. From the beginning of the American Republic, arguments over which policies (e.g., education, police, welfare, and so on) were properly legislated at the national level, and which were governed by the regional governments have permeated American society and politics. Generally, the "Federalists" (George Washington, Alexander Hamilton, and John Adams) favored more power and control from the central regime, while the "Anti-Federalists," or "States Rights" advocated, resisted centralized government in favor of more power at the local and state levels of government. Thomas Jefferson was of the latter school: he wanted the small regional governments to conduct most of the people's business, reserving the national government for foreign and interstate concerns (the military, international trade, state boundary controversies, and so forth). He based this premise on the democratic belief that a government closer to the citizens is more effective and responsive. Jefferson started his theory of a republic at the smallest local level of government or "wards." A ward is like a town, village, or small rural area of five to six square miles with a few hundred citizens. Jefferson's ward districts bore a resemblance to the ideal polis, which strove to realize man's social nature through direct citizen participation in local community life.[3] As such, these classical republics were limited in size and population, so Jefferson adapted them to the large American continent through a new theory of representative democracy which grew out of, rather than competed with, ward divisions.[4] American democracy was supposed to start at the local community level where every citizen could participate in some form of government (council, jury, law enforcement, care of the poor, e.g.), thus developing his natural social talents and loyalty. Then, out of the best local leaders, representatives would be elected to serve at more centralized (county, state, national) governments. The "ward republics" though were always the core of American federalism, for Jefferson.

Declaring the wards to be "small republics," created out of the smallest existing jurisdictions, the counties, Jefferson provided a precise definition of his notion of these political entities when he wrote: "Were I to assign to this term a precise and definite idea, I would say, purely and simply, it means a government by its citizens in mass, acting directly and personally, according to rules established by the majority; and that every other government is more or less republican in proportion as it has in its composition more or less of this ingredient of the direct action of the citizens."[5] That was his idea of a republic. Direct participation by citizens in politics.

Among those things which Jefferson considered immediately relevant to ward residents, in addition to the elementary schools, and, he thought, within their competence, were "care of their poor, their roads, police, elections, the nomination of jurors, administration of justice in small cases, elementary exercises of militia and all those concerns which, being under their eye, they would better manage than the larger republics of the county or state."[6] That is, a large portion of rule would occur at local government levels.

Such minor republics, which Jefferson saw as similar to New England townships, were for him "the wisest invention ever devised by the wit of man for the perfect exercise of self-government, and for its preservation,"[7] because "by making every citizen an acting member of the government, and in the offices nearest and most interesting to him, will attach him by his strongest feelings to the independence of his country, and its republican Constitution."[8] While he saw direct participation in local political life drawing out citizens' affections for their community, or public virtue, Jefferson also regarded the wards' small size as contributing to intelligent public deliberation and the development of citizens' minds, as evidenced by his repeated plea: "reduce your legislature to a convenient number for full but orderly discussion."[9] Public discourse had an educative effect, for Jefferson.

While also cultivating citizens' hearts and minds, classical participatory democracy, he thought, would also prevent the degeneration of the state into a tyranny; for Jefferson warned: "If [the people] become inattentive to the public affairs, you and I, Congress and Assemblies, Judges and Governors, shall all become wolves."[10] In other words, for Jefferson, democratically educated citizens are the best insurance against government violations of individual natural rights: "when there shall not be a man in the State who will not be a member of some one of its councils great or small, he will let the heart be torn out of his body sooner than his power be wrested from him by a Caesar or a Bonaparte."[11] Active involvement produces wise, strong citizens, for Jefferson.

In spite of Jefferson's devotion to small, classical republics, he was not blind to their geographical limitations. "Such a government," he wrote, "is evidently restrained to very narrow limits of space and population."[12] In a country the size of the United States, Jefferson conceived of a representative democracy as a natural extension of ward republican government. "This I should consider as the nearest approach to a pure republic, which is practicable on a large scale of country or population."[13] However, unlike the immediate structure of ward republics, which might benefit from notions borrowed from Ancient Greece, this representative adaptation of local participatory democracy to a large nation required for Jefferson entirely original ideas: "The full experiment of a government democratical, but representative, was and is still reserved for us…this…has rendered useless almost everything written before on the structure of government; and in a great measure, relieves our regret, if the political writings of Aristotle, or of any other ancient, have been lost, or are unfaithfully rendered or explained to us."[14] America was not an ancient, but a Modern regime.

Jefferson provided an entirely new political theory; his original theory, though, designed for the unique conditions of America, still drew heavily from the past. He constructed America's larger, representative republic out of the smaller, participatory ones, insisting that "these little republics would be the main strength of the great one."[15] The means of connecting the local ward republics with the increasingly centralized ones is simple: its general principle is that the elementary republics of the wards, the county and state republics, and the republic of the Union, would form a system of fundamental checks and balances for the government,[16] founded on every citizen personally taking part in the administration of the public affairs, and forming a pyramid of republics.[17]

This Jeffersonian standard of American federalism provided the basis for his critique of what became the existing structure of American constitutional government. What remains for him of republicanism after the Federalists' manipulation of Constitution and Court "is not the fruit of our Constitution, but has prevailed in spite of it."[18] He was disappointed by what became of American politics, as Atatürk was later sometimes disappointed with weaknesses in the Turkish republic.

So, Jefferson regarded the classical ward republics as "the key-stone of the arch of our government."[19] His concept of small participatory democracies constituted his mature political theory, and his conception of human nature as naturally social and requiring the exercise of one's moral and political faculties for individual development and the public good, contrasted with his earlier, revolutionary theory premised in Lockean liberalism. Yet, just as his revolutionary appeal to Lockean categories defended autonomous, republican legislatures, Jefferson's later appeal to classical republican politics, he believed, would enhance the preservation of fundamental rights and liberties. From his mature perspective, Jefferson did not emphasize the individual's freedom from social ties, but rather, insisted that the absence of an active public realm cultivating man's social and moral capacities would not lead to freedom and happiness but to "sinning and suffering." Apart from a meaningful public life, Jefferson believed, individuals would be reduced to miserable "automatons" devoid of true, intelligent choice.[20] This left Jefferson, just two years before his death at age 83, still working for an amendment to Virginia's Constitution dividing the counties into ward republics.[21] The American historical tendency to shift political power from the state and local governments to the central national regime violates Jefferson's conception of a republic, but the flexibility of the United States Constitution has allowed frequent returns to more state autonomy and authority, as recently as the late 1990s.

Jefferson involved Lockean language reminiscent of his earlier revolutionary writings in defense of the sovereign autonomy of state and local republics against the encroachment of a distant centralized and what he saw as corrupt regimes. While in the 1770s, that distant, oppressive regime was in London, usurping the legitimate rule of the colonial legislatures, in the 1790s and 1820s, it was in Washington, D.C., where under the control of the "Federalists," it was usurping the legitimate rule of the state and local republics.[22] Even where Jefferson's classical republicanism is most obvious—in his conception of the autonomy of classical participatory republics governed by an economically independent, educated, and politically active citizenry, promoting public virtue within a balanced, mixed constitution—we find it complemented by a modified Lockean liberalism declaring the rights of equal and independent legislatures. He blends philosophical traditions, just as Atatürk's republican ideology was eclectic and flexible.

Jefferson's standard for American federalism was a functional one: each tier of government was to perform those functions it performed best. In Jefferson's eighteenth-century view, this standard distributed most domestic concerns to the state and local governments, restricting the national government primarily to foreign relations.[23]

> [T]he way to have good and safe government, is not to trust it all to one, but to divide it among the many, distributing to every one exactly the functions he is competent to. Let the national government be entrusted with the defense of the nation, and its foreign and federal relations; the State governments with the civil rights, laws, police, and administration of what concerns the State generally; the counties with the local concerns of the counties; and each ward direct the interests within itself. It is by dividing and subdividing these republics from the great national one down through all its subordinations, until it ends in the administration of every man's farm by himself; by placing under everyone what his own eye may superintend, that all will be done for the best.[24]

This distribution of the government into the national (one) the states (few), and the localities (many) formed Jefferson's true conception of a balanced, mixed Constitution and Federalism.

Hence, Jefferson's federal republic was a pyramid founded upon the local ward republics, followed by county and state republics, and crowned by the national republic, which formed a graduation of authorities, constituting a good system of checks and balances.[25] Hence, Jefferson's famous inaugural phrase, "We are all republicans—we are federalists,"[26] became more than just a conciliatory remark; it provided a concise description of his idea of American federalism, elaborated in a political diary of the period: "I fondly hope, 'we may now truly say, we are all republicans, all federalists,' and that the motto of the standard to which our country will forever rally, will be, 'federal union, and republican government.'"[27] The extent to which Jefferson subordinated the "federal" to the "republic" is illustrated by his insistence that this pyramid of republics be "cemented" by direct participation of every citizen in the political like of the country.[28] Local Ward democracy created and strengthened the larger republic.

Because this classical democracy in the ward republics constituted the foundation of the Federated Union, and the local and state republics were charged with most domestic political concerns, the national government was properly relegated, for Jefferson, to international affairs. While direct control of internal politics (cultivation and exercise of man's moral sense, effective ordering of education, economics, and leadership, etc.) made classical participatory politics appropriate to state and local regimes, the distant and removed quality of the national government made liberal political principles (limited government, delegated authority) appropriate to the central federal government. This explains why Jefferson, after developing an extensive and even somewhat intrusive role for the local ward democracies (strictly regulating education, politics, economics, and leadership) nevertheless characterized good federal government as very limited, as shown in his remark in the first inaugural address: "a wise and frugal government, which shall restrain men from injuring one another, which shall leave them otherwise free to regulate their own pursuits of industry and improvement."[29] Jefferson was content to limit the national government in liberal fashion because he was confident that Americans' political life was mostly best conducted in the local and state republics. As he insisted in his first Presidential message to Congress, "the states themselves have principal care of our persons, our property, and our reputation, constituting the great field of human concerns"[30] He believed in States Rights.

Not the least of these human concerns for Jefferson was the cultivation of each individual's moral sense, that highest faculty of man, which required the intimacy of local education and political participation for its development and exercise. Therefore, when Jefferson perceived the federal government encroaching upon the local ward and state republics through increasing involvement in domestic concerns, his assaults on that national authority came in the language of Locke and called for a restrained, limited government in a manner reminiscent of his revolutionary writings directed against the British Parliament's similar encroachment on the local colonial legislatures. In both instances, the freedom defended with Lockean rhetoric was the freedom of small communities to exercise self-government, and of individuals to realize their social nature through participation in and control over their collective lives. Since Jefferson regarded an economically independent citizenry as requisite to a virtuous republic that was not only a defense of political balance, but also a defense of evenly distributed property against Hamilton's financial schemes that would concentrate wealth in the hands of a few. Centralized regimes often became corrupt financially—leaders stealing money and impoverishing the masses.

In December of 1825, Jefferson wrote "The Solemn Declaration and Protest of the Commonwealth of Virginia, On the Principles of the Constitution of the United States of America, and on the Violations of Them" (134–136). Its liberal language echoes Jefferson's first Declaration of Independence: He again refers to "free and independent" states, to the "usurpation" of their sovereign authority by a centralized power, and he appeals to his "federal brethren" to discontinue these encroachments while noting the threat to "life, liberty and property" implied in their invasion of state and local democracy.[31] He hales a clarion call against tyranny.

A similarity of this second declaration with its revolutionary predecessor is apparent even in its preamble: "The States in North America which confederated to establish their independence of the government of Great Britain, of which Virginia was one, became, on acquisition, free and independent States, and as such authorized to constitute governments, each for itself, in such form as it thought best."[32] After recounting the historical origins of the states' independence from Great Britain, Jefferson provides his view of the creation of a new central authority in America, through the compact made by those independent states: "They entered into a compact (which is called the Constitution of the United States of America), by which they agreed to unite in a single government as to their relations with each other, and with foreign nations.... They retained at the same time, each to itself, the other rights of independent government, comprehending their domestic interests" (134). However, as the British Parliament before it, this newly created central federal government gradually extended its authority into the economic, social, and political prerogatives of the smaller republics: "[t]he federal branch has assumed in some cases, and claimed in others, a right of enlarging its own powers...which this assembly [of Virginia] does declare to be usurpations of the power retained to the independent [State] branches."[33]

Like the British Parliament, it was not just the expansion of the federal government which threatened local democracy, it was the corruption of politics itself, following from the commercial venality to which distant regimes were particularly susceptible. It threatened to poison public virtue by removing the government from direct citizen accountability and delivering it to corrupt speculators and merchants. Political corruption originally attributed to the "greed and avarice" of English merchants,[34] Jefferson now saw emanating from "the wealthy aristocrats, the [American] merchants connected closely with England [and] the newly created paper fortunes.[35] So, Jefferson wrote of the High Federalists, and their leader Alexander Hamilton, "all the administrative laws were shaped on the model of England...and [were] to be warped, in practice, into all the principles and pollutions of their favorite English model....[For] Hamilton was not only a monarchist, but for a monarchy bottomed in corruption."[36] Fiscal corruption robbed the citizenry of government funds and soiled public virtue and patriotism.

Jefferson's own definition of "corruption" as "a legislature legislating for its own interests, in opposition to those of the people" followed Aristotle's definition of a corrupt regime ruling for its private good rather than for the public good.[37] Such corruption, for Jefferson, flourished in distant regimes where leaders were less directly accountable to the people. There a government might be captured by commercial interests, who because of their necessity to constantly be occupied with private gain, were not well suited to protecting the good of the whole society, the public virtue. Jefferson's system of participatory republics, producing both an educated electorate and a natural aristocracy capable of perceiving the good of the whole society, was designed to diminish the possibility of rule by the "pseudo-aristocracy" of wealth which brought such corruption to the public realm. The real threat of this political and financial corruption to the public virtue was the concentration of wealth and political power which would effectively destroy the economically independent and politically active citizenry whose function was necessary to a classical republic.[38] Just as Atatürk later encouraged governmental economic policy benefiting the whole of Turkey, Jefferson wanted lean, honest government.

In the early Republic, though, American federalism developed in a different way from Jefferson's ideal vision, breeding an isolated and venal federal legislature which Jefferson identified largely with Hamilton's fiscal system and corruption. The Secretary of the Treasury's plans for reimbursing holders of government bonds, assuming the state's debts, and establishing a National Bank, all revealed this commercial corruption. Jefferson regarded this as a "base scramble" for public funds and misappropriated political power, a "detestable game" of "greedy creditors and speculators" whose manipulations of the public trust allowed "immense sums to be filched from the poor and ignorant."[39] Atatürk's resistance to political leaders stealing public funds resembles Jefferson's concern. Worse, Hamilton's corrupting fiscal policy derived from a corrupt political theory, which strove to govern men by appealing solely to their selfish interests, and expected to somehow create a just and orderly society out of the aggregate of those interests, rather than acknowledging and cultivating the highest faculty in man: his social, ethical nature. For Jefferson, Hamilton's policies came directly from this base, Hobbesian view of human nature. Hamilton's fiscal system "had two objects; first, as a puzzle, to exclude popular understanding and inquiry; second, as a machine for the corruption of the legislature; for he avowed the opinion that man could be governed by one of two motives only, force or interest; force he observed, in this country was out of the question, and the interests, therefore, of the member [of Congress] must be laid hold of, to keep the legislative unison with the executive" (1208). Hamilton's politics were not "evil" as such; they were merely the logical extension of a psychology that had dominated modernity since Hobbes, conceiving of man as only a material individual, seeking nothing but self-preservation. Jefferson pointed out what happened: "And with grief and shame it must be acknowledged that [Hamilton's] machine was not without effect; that even in this, the birth of our government, some members were found sordid enough to bend their duty to their interests, and to look after personal rather than public good."[40] The temptations of power always corrupt some political leaders with greed to the harm of the common people.

The ultimate effect of this corrupt system, premised in a corrupt political theory founded on a corrupt psychology, was to debase political leaders and followers alike. Instead of the rule of the patriotic natural aristocracy of wisdom and virtue, emanating from participatory ward republics, Hamilton's system and the perversions it symbolized, issued forth the rule of "the stock-jobbing herd,"[41] reducing public good to the sum of private goods. This, in turn, replaced the, active, intelligent citizenry of Jefferson's vision, with an alienated, passive and dangerously ignorant populace obsessed with private ambition. Jefferson blamed this dismemberment of the body politic on policies committed to withdrawing the people from honest business pursuits and encouraging them to "occupy themselves and their capitals in a species of gambling, destructive of morality, and which has introduced its poison into the government itself" (1216). Once government corruption spread, all of society became corrupt.

Rather than the virtue and wisdom created by the democracy of the ward republics flowing up to the higher regions of American federalism Jefferson sadly observed the corruption of Hamilton's federal government filtering down to pollute the state and local regimes. His hope for the American republic remained, however, for an enlightened, moral citizenry governing for the common good.

Atatürk

The Turkish Republic turned a feudal, illiterate, impoverished autocratic empire into a modern, educated, prosperous, and largely democratic nation. As Atatürk's biographer Lord Kinross noted of its leader: "He had saved and revived Turkey; he had transformed a crumbling straggling empire, beset by enemies, into a compact homogeneous state, recognized by potential friends."[42] To accomplish such a radical transformation of Turkish society Atatürk often used strong methods. He often violated abstract democratic principles to preserve and nurture the Republic. Like Jefferson's attitude towards the original inhabitants of Louisiana,[43] Atatürk saw that the majority of Turkish citizens in the 1920s and 1930s were not capable of self-government and needed years of education, economic prosperity, and independence to become fully democratic. Atatürk's solution to these needed reforms of Turkish society to prepare it for democracy came to be known as Kemalism. The principles of Kemalism were (1) Republicanism; (2) Nationalism; (3) Populism; (4) Statism; (5) Secularism; and (6) Reformism.[44] These Kemalist ideals, which resemble in many ways the spirit of Western and Jeffersonian democracy, brought a medieval, Islamic monarchy into the modern European republican world.

Republicanism meant government through the will of the people, parliamentary elections, rotation of office, and popular sovereignty. The beginning of the Republic in Turkey is usually dated at April 23, 1920, with the opening of the Grand National Assembly in Ankara. Although it would be decades before the full realization of a Western-style parliamentary republic would be achieved (multiparty democracy, constitutional supremacy; individual rights to complete freedom of conscience, speech, press, religious liberty and due process of law), Atatürk began the arduous task of transforming the old Ottoman Empire into a modern, liberal Western society.

Nationalism meant an independent, powerful country free from foreign domination. Unlike the multicultural Ottoman Empire, the Turkish nation is distinct in culture, but it pledged to tolerate diversity in culture and religion and respect individual freedom and conscience.

Populism means democratic control by the people of internal politics through the rule of law. Self-government, popularly elected leaders, and regular elections constitute "populism" in the Turkish sense.

Statism refers to the mixture of private property/free enterprise economics with government control of major industries and regulation of the overall economy for the good of the whole country. Today, this "mixed economy" of capitalism and socialism dominates in modern, Western societies.

Secularism means the formal, legal separation of religion from politics, the end of the domination of the state by Islamic officials, and the individual freedom of conscience to believe, worship, and communicate religious truths as the individual understands them. Such liberty of religion implies the freedom to learn of all faiths, to seek God's guidance in knowing His Truth, and sharing it with others without fear of persecution or injury. The premise of this is that such individual searching after God's Truth and voluntary faith in God is pleasing to God, while forced adherence to a certain religion is not really pleasing to God.

Reformism is the changing of Turkish society to conform with modern civilization and progress. Kemal's reforms included granting equal legal rights to women; adopting the Western justice code; public education; using the Latin (rather than Arabic) alphabet; abolition of titles; adoption of Western time standards, calendar, and measures; abolition of rural tithes and traditional religious dress codes (123, 121, 143.). Together, these reforms radically transformed Turkey from an impoverished, isolated society to a prosperous, democratic culture integrated into the modern, civilized world.

However, Atatürk's political principles did not take effect immediately. They took a few generations to become embedded in the Turkish culture and psyche. They required "the talents of a reformer, a prophet, a statesman," and Kemal Atatürk became all those things.[45] He led the early, fledging Turkish Republic with a dedicated mind and strong hand. He used a new Parliament, "packed by himself, and a new party, of which he was the founder and leader," as Lord Kinross described it (378).

At the first Grand National Assembly, Atatürk told an Austrian journalist that Turkey was now a Republic, that its sovereignty belonged to the people and that "there is no difference between all the Republics of Europe and America" and that of the new Turkish state (378–379). This was still a radical idea in Turkey; many representatives in the Assembly wanted a Constitutional monarchy with the Sultan remaining monarch or the Caliph being President. Atatürk simply proclaimed a secular Republic: "The form of the Government of the Turkish state is a Republic," he said. Its President would be head of state, elected by the Assembly, and would appoint the Prime Minister who would appoint the other ministers with the approval of the Assembly (380). In October 1923, Atatürk was elected President of this new Turkish Republic by the National Assembly. He had transformed a major portion of the world.

Like Jefferson, who occupied positions of "Founder" of American Independence, United States President and Leader of the mass Democratic Republican Party, Atatürk soon was a triplicate ruler: President, head of Cabinet, and head of the only political party. A friend compared him to the Christian Trinity God (Father, Son, and Holy Spirit)—all powerful; and Kemal replied, "It is true, but don't tell anyone" (381).

Atatürk's political colleagues, like the American Federalists, (who once accused Jefferson of being "The Grand Turk")[46] began to be concerned about the concentration of power in one man's hands. They responded by organizing various opposition Parties to Atatürk's People's Republican Party. The Progressive Party strove to be a permanent minority opposition Party, curbing the dominant Party's power and protecting rights of free speech and press. Atatürk was concerned that this party could join with the military to upset his government, but later he was stung by Western criticism of Turkey's one-party government and he encouraged Opposition.[47] He organized and encouraged two-party government, but his powerful influence continued to be felt. As long as the "Father of Turkey" remained alive, a genuine independent regime apart from his dynamic leadership was impossible. A journalist recorded the scene of the Assembly operating under Atatürk's dominating gaze and overpowering personality:

> The Gazi [Atatürk] sat in his private box watching the tilting between the Government and the Opposition . . .beaming when a telling point was scored, frowning when a point was awkwardly handled. Gillespie says it reminded him of nothing so much as a proud father watching his sons competing in two opposing debating teams (453).

As long as Atatürk was alive, his strong and dynamic leadership would prevent the Turkish Republic from operating apart from the Founder of its Independence and uniqueness. Although a domineering Father, Atatürk wanted his children to grow up to be strong, intelligent, independent republican citizens, taking their place in the modern world as a respectable, accomplished nation.

Notes

1. Morison, *The Oxford History of the American People*, 1:394.
2. See Garrett Ward Sheldon, *The Political Philosophy of James Madison* (Baltimore: Johns Hopkins University Press, 2000).
3. Jefferson's response to Montesquieu's theories revolve around his attempt to adapt classical small republics to a large country, which the French philosopher insisted could not be done (see Jefferson, *Commonplace Book*, 32–33, 267). When Jefferson served in France, he also found that parties favorable to monarchy cited Montesquieu, which cooled Jefferson's attitude. Jefferson retained of Montesquieu his most classical republican qualities: emphasis on civic virtue, public participation, small republics, public education, and an economic dimension to
4. Cf. Aristotle, *Politics*, book 1, ch. 6, 9, 114, 121; that Jefferson was familiar with Aristotle's *Politics* is evidenced by the presence of the book on his bedside table late in his life (see Merrill D. Peterson, *Thomas Jefferson and the New Nation* [New York: Oxford University Press, 1970], 1008).
5. Jefferson to John Taylor, May 28, 1816, *The Writings of Thomas Jefferson*, 20 Vols., ed. Albert Ellery Bergh (Washington, D.C.: Thomas Jefferson Memorial Association, 1904–1905), hereafter WTJ. 15: 19; to Samuel Kercheval, July 12, 1816, 33 ("let it be agreed that a government is republican in proportion as every member composing it has his equal voice in the direction of its concerns"). Cf. Montesquieu, "The people, in whom the supreme power resides, ought to have the management of everything within their reach; that which exceeds their abilities must be conducted by their minister" (*Spirit of the Laws*, 1:9).
6. Jefferson to John Adams, October 28, 1813, *The Adams–Jefferson Letters*, 2 Vols., ed. Lester J. Capon (Chapel Hill: University of North Carolina Press, 1959), hereafter A-JL. 2: 390; also to Samuel Kercheval, July 12, 1816, *WTJ*, 15:37. Jefferson's vision of "social welfare," largely detailed in his *Notes on the State of Virginia*, differs substantially from both contemporary (late twentieth century) national welfare programs and the local private charities which existed throughout America prior to the New Deal. While not as technologically sophisticated as the former, they seem rather closer in humanitarianism to the latter, while still being publicly supported. For example, care of the poor, aged, and sick was to be publicly subsidized (through ward revenues) but privately administered, always attempting to supplement the family and friendship relations that already existed. The sick who had no family or friends with whom to stay were to be placed in the home of a "good farmer," whose family environment Jefferson considered more conducive to healing than an impersonal hospital: "Nature and kind nursing save a much greater proportion in our plain way, at a smaller expense, and with less abuse" (in *The Complete Jefferson*, ed. Saul K. Padover (New York: Tudor, 1943), 658).
7. Jefferson to Samuel Kercheval, July 12, 1816, *WTJ*, 15:38.
8. Ibid., 37. Cf. this to Aristotle's definition of citizenship: "there are different kinds of citizens, but…a citizen in the fullest sense is one who has a share in the privileges of rule" (*Politics*, book 3, ch. 5, 112).

9. Jefferson to Samuel Kercheval, July 12, 1816, *WTJ*, 15:36. This also reflects Jefferson's mature appreciation of classical political theory. Other evidence for Jefferson's attitudes toward modern conflictual and ancient consensual politics appears in his *Autobiography*, where he contrasts the American Congress's "very contentious...morbid rage of debate" with the young French aristocrats in Paris during the late 1780s, whose "coolness and candor of argument...logical reasoning and chaste eloquence, disfigured by no gaudy tinsel of rhetoric or declamation, and truly worthy of being placed in parallel with the finest dialogues of antiquity, as handed to us by Xenophon, Plato, and Cicero" (70, 114).
10. Jefferson to Dol. Edward Carrington, January 16, 1787, *WTJ*, 5:58.
11. Jefferson to Joseph C. Cabell, Feb. 2, 1816, *WTJ*, 14: 422. The same argument for the strength of republican government occurs in Jefferson's "First Inaugural Address": "It is the only one where every man, at the call of the laws, would fly to the standard of the law, and would meet invasion of the public order as his own personal concern" (in *The Complete Jefferson*, 385).
12. Jefferson to John Taylor, May 28, 1816, *WTJ*, 15:19. Cf. Aristotle's observation in *Politics*, book 7, ch. 5, 266; and Montesquieu's *Spirit of the Laws*, 1:120: "It is natural for a republic to have only a small territory; otherwise it cannot long subsist. In an extensive republic there are men of large fortunes, and consequently of less moderation.

    In an extensive republic the public good is sacrificed to a thousand private views; it is subordinate to exceptions, and depends on accidents. In a small one, the interest of the public is more obvious, better understood, and more within the reach of every citizen; abuses have less extent, and, of course, are less protected."
13. Jefferson to John Taylor, *WTJ*.
14. Jefferson to Isaac Tiffany, August 26, 1816, ibid., 66; though even here, evidence exists showing that Jefferson's idea of the states' "compact" into a federated Union may have been an attempt at replicating the "confederation" of city-states *Commonplace Book*, entries 717, 729.
15. Jefferson to Governor John Tyler, May 26, 1810, *WTJ*, 12:394.
16. Jefferson to Joseph C. Cabell, February 2, 1816, *WTJ*, 14:422.
17. Jefferson to Samuel Kercheval, July 12, 1816, *WTJ*, 15:35.
18. Jefferson to Samuel Kercheval, July 12, 1816, *WTJ*, 15:35.
19. Jefferson to John Adams, Oct. 28, 1813, *A-JL*, 2:390.
20. Jefferson to Samuel Kercheval, July 12, 1816, *WTJ*, 15:40.
21. By the time of his retirement, Jefferson was not optimistic over the likelihood of reforming the American federal structure, believing that the "golden moment is past for reforming these heresies" of the republican creed (to John Taylor, May 28, 1816, *WTJ*, 15:22).
22. J. G. A. Pocock, "Machiavelli, Harrington, and English Political Ideologies in the Eighteenth Century," *William and Mary Quarterly* 22 (October 1965): 549-83.
23. Jefferson to Joseph C. Cabell, February 2, 1816, *WTJ*, 14: 421. Jefferson's criticism of Aristotle and Montesquieu was not over their conceptions of man's social nature or the need for political participation by a virtuous citzenry, but rather their contention that such a classical republic could only exist in a small nation, while Jefferson

believed that it could exist in a large nation if connected in this way to successively more centralized republics. Of Aristotle and the Greeks, Jefferson wrote, "They know no medium between a democracy (the only pure republic, but impractical beyond the limits of a town) and an abandonment of themselves to an aristocracy, or a tyranny independent of the people. It seems not to have occurred that where the citizens can not meet to transact their business in person, they alone have the right to choose the agents who shall transact it; and that in this way a republican, or popular government, of the second grade of purity, may be exercised over any extent of country" (to Isaac Tiffany, 1816, *WTJ*, 7:32).

24. Jefferson, *The Commonplace Book of Thomas Jefferson: A Repertory of His Ideas on Government*, ed. Gilbert Chinard (Baltimore: Johns Hopkins University Press, 1926), 32–34, 37, 267.
25. Jefferson to Joseph C. Cabell, Feb. 2, 1816, *WTJ*, 14:422. See C. B. Macpherson, *The Life and Times of Liberal Democracy* (New York: Oxford University Press, 1977), 108–109.
26. Jefferson, "First Inaugural Address," *The Complete Jefferson,* ed. Saul K. Padover (New York: Tudor, 1943), 385.
27. See Jefferson, *The Anas*, *CJ*, 1212–13.
28. Jefferson to Samuel Kercheval, July 12, 1816, *WTJ*, 15:38.
29. In Jefferson, *The Complete Jefferson*, 386.
30. In Jefferson, *The Complete Jefferson*, 390. See also The Kentucky Resolutions (1798), in which Jefferson makes the distinction between the national and the state governments in these terms: "a general government for special purposes—delegated to that government certain definite powers, reserving, each state to itself the residuary mass of right to their own self-government" (*The Complete Jefferson*, 129).
31. *The Complete Jefferson*, Cf. Jefferson's language in the original Declaration of Independence: "free and independent" states; "usurpation;" "British brethren;" "life, liberty."
32. Thomas Jefferson, The Solemn Declaration and Protest of the Commonwealth of Virginia, on the Principles of the Constitution of the United States of America, and on the Violations of Them (December 1825), *The Complete Jefferson*, 134.
33. Thomas Jefferson, The Solemn Declaration and Protest of the Commonwealth of Virginia, on the Principles of the Constitution of the United States of America, and on the Violations of Them (December 1825), *The Complete Jefferson*, 135. Jefferson saw this usurpation in the federal government generally, but especially in the executive and judicial branches (see Murrin, "The Great Inversion," 405–06, 427; Robert E. Shalhope, "Thomas Jefferson's Republicanism and Antebellum Southern Thought," *Journal of Southern History* 42 (November 1976): 545.
34. See Thomas Jefferson, *A Summary View of the Rights of British America, The Papers of Thomas Jefferson*, 60 vols., ed. Julian Boyd (Princeton: Princeton University Press, 1950), 1:124, 127.
35. Jefferson, *The Anas*, 1258.
36. Jefferson, *The Anas*, 1210–11, 1226 (Jefferson concluded that "Hamilton was, indeed, a singular character").

37. Aristotle, *The Politics*, book 3, chs. 6, 7.

38. As Jefferson wrote of the Federalists: They wish "to lessen the dependence of the Executive and of one branch of the Legislature on the people, some by making them hold for life, some hereditary, and some even giving the Executive an influence by patronage or corruption over the remaining popular branch, so as to reduce the elective franchise to its minimum" (to J. F. Mercer, 1804, *WTJ*, 4:563). Cf. Harrington, *Oceana*, ed. S. B. Liljegen (Westport, Conn.: Hyperion Press, 1979), 37:

> such (except it be in a city that has little or no land, and whose revenue is in trade) as in the population or balance of dominion or property in land, such is the nature of the empire.
>
> If one man be sole landlord of a territory, or overbalance the people, for example three parts in four...his empire is absolute monarchy.
>
> If the few or a nobility, or a nobility with the clergy be landlords, or overbalance the people to the like proportion, it makes the *Gothic* balan...and the empire is mix'd monarchy.... And if the whole people be landlords, or hold the lands so divided among them, that no one man, or number of men, within the compass of the *few* or *aristocracy*, overbalance them, the empire (without the interposition of force) is a commonwealth.

39. Jefferson, *The Anas*, 1208, 1246. Cf. Bolingbroke's characterization of Walpole's government dominated by the "the usurer and the stockjobbers...those leeches who fill themselves continually wit the blood of the nation" (in Isaac Kramnick, *Bolingbroke and His Circle* [Cambridge: Harvard University Press, 1968], 37). Jefferson went so far as to advocate secession by the southern states rather than be dominated by the financial policies of the Northeast:

> Every society has a right to fix the fundamental principles of its association, and to say to all individuals, that, if they contemplate pursuits beyond the limits of these principles, and involving dangers which the society chooses to avoid, they must go somewhere else for their exercise; that we want no citizens, and still less ephemeral and pseudo-citizens, on such terms. We may exclude them from our territory, as we do persons infected with disease. Such is the situation of our country. We have the most abundant resources of happiness without ourselves, which we may enjoy in peace and safety, without permitting a few citizens, infected with the mania of rambling and gambling, to bring danger on the great mass engaged in innocent and safe pursuits at home. In your letter to Fisk, you have fairly stated the alternatives between which we are to choose: 1, licentious commerce and gambling speculations for a few, with eternal war for the many; or, 2, restricted commerce, peace, and steady occupations for all. If any State in the Union will declare that it prefers separation with the first alternative, to a continuance in union without it, I have no hesitation in saying, "let us separate." I would rather the States would withdraw, which are for unlimited commerce and war, and confederate with those alone which are for peace and agriculture. (To William Crawford, June 20, 1816, *WTJ*, 11:538)

This alienation form northern commercial corruption extended to southerners being educated in New England, which was one of the reasons Jefferson wanted to establish the University of Virginia,, providing southern gentlemen with an alternative to Princeton or Harvard (see Shalhope, "Thomas Jefferson's Republicanism," 552).

40. Jefferson, Jefferson elsewhere described Mr. Hamilton as "a man whose history, from the moment history can stoop to notice him, is a tissue of machinations against the liberty of the country which has not only received and given him bread but heaped honors on his head" (quoted in Merrill D. Peterson, *Thomas Jefferson and the New Nation* [New York: Oxford University Press, 1970], 474). The evidence for Hamilton's uncommonly close ties with English mercantilist fortunes and their Parliament was pervasive for Jefferson (see *The Anas,* 1272, 1274, 1276, 1279).
41. Jefferson, *The Anas*, 1210.
42. Kinross, *Atatürk*, 377.
43. Sheldon, *The Political Philosophy of Thomas Jefferson*, 98.
44. Ozel, *Atatürk*, 143.
45. Kinross, 377.
46. Sheldon, 98.
47. Kinross, 450

CHAPTER FOUR

RELIGIOUS FREEDOM

Jefferson

Thomas Jefferson was a devout Christian, but he insisted that religious freedom was essential to true religion. The individual person must have complete liberty of conscience to investigate different religious faiths and to decide which he or she believed was true. Only a religious belief arrived at freely is pleasing to God. Any forced religion is false religion. The society that coerces religious belief through threats or political penalties is not faithful to God, but breeds fear and hypocrisy. True religion, knowledge, and love of God, requires freedom of inquiry and liberty of conscience. That is why Jefferson opposed the official state religion—it imposed a formal, legalistic religion on everyone. True faith, for Jefferson, would be arrived at by patient, serious inquiry, tested by Scripture and life experience, not enforced by law. In the end, Jefferson believed true religion would spread and flourish in such a free atmosphere, civilizing society and pleasing the Almighty. He hoped and believed that such religious freedom would further the ethics of Jesus—love, repentance, compassion, peace, and forgiveness—producing a moral society in America and helping democracy work.

Jefferson himself was deeply religious. He studied the Bible all his life and contributed to many religious societies and institutions.[1] He enjoyed church music and religious art. Jefferson summarized Christianity as "(1) Faith, (2) Repentance. That faith is everywhere explained to be a belief that Jesus was the Messiah.... Repentance was to be proved sincere by good works...a system of morality, delivered on such authority as to give it sanction...an inducement to a pious life, by revealing clearly a future existence in bliss, and that it was to be the reward of the virtuous" (27). To be genuine, religious belief had to be voluntary, as "the rights of conscience...are answerable...[only] to our God" (29). Restrictions on religious freedom, like a state imposed religion, only led to persecution and violence in the name of God, which was the greatest blasphemy. "Millions of innocent men, women, and children...have been burnt, tortured, fined and imprisoned [and] what has been the effect of coercion? To make one-half the world fools, and the other half hypocrites" (28). For Jefferson, God and true faith did not need official state religion; rather, the best religion flourished in an atmosphere of freedom and tolerance. The test of true religion was how people act; as Jesus said, faith is displayed by its fruits, or the exhibition of Godly values: kindness, mercy, love, forgiveness, and charity. The best society encourages free investigation and discussion of all religious faiths and protects believers in minority religions and those who change their religions in adulthood. All individuals are answerable to God only for their beliefs. Each person has the moral responsibility to investigate all religions to see to which one God is leading him or her. Social, cultural, or political pressure to believe a certain truth about God, or to restrict honest searching for God's truth, prevent true religion from spreading. Persecution of any religious group is not pleasing to God. America could only be a successful democracy and prosperous economy if it allowed religious freedom. Peaceful competition among religious groups would keep them honest and humble. A religious monopoly in a society would breed pride, ignorance, arrogance, and unjust persecution. However, respect for others' beliefs and openness to alternative doctrines could foster a healthy, peaceful, and just society.

His conception of a virtuous American republic presumed the existence of a social ethics appropriate to a naturally social being possessing a divinely ordained moral sense. This conformed to man's natural sympathies and fostered a sense of duty to his fellow citizens. As Jefferson wrote to John Adams:

> If by *religion*, we are to understand *sectarian dogmas*, in which no two of them agree, then your exclamation...is just, "that this would be the best of all possible worlds, if there were no religion in it." But if the moral precepts, innate in man, and made a part of his physical condition, as necessary of a social being, if the sublime doctrines...taught us by Jesus of Nazareth in which all agree, constitute true religion, then, without it, this would be, as you again say, "something not fit to be named, even indeed a Hell."[2]

Jefferson regarded man as a social and political being, requiring participation in the human community for his full development and happiness, and in need of an ethical creed which enhanced relations among individuals and promoted social harmony.[3] It was into the world of classical self-perfection, insisted Jefferson, that Jesus gave a moral philosophy suited to man's true, God-given nature: "His moral doctrines, relating to kindred and friends were more pure and perfect than those of the most correct of philosophers and...went far beyond in inculcating universal philanthropy not only to kindred and friends, to neighbors and countrymen, but to all mankind, gathering all into one family, under the bond of love, charity, peace, common wants and common aids.... [Herein lies] the peculiar superiority of the system of Jesus over all others."[4]

Jesus Christ's ethical teachings of love, repentence, and forgiveness, of universal brotherhood and charity provided, for Jefferson, "the most sublime and benevolent code of morals which has ever been offered to man" for his life in society.[5] "Epictetus and Epicurus gave laws for governing ourselves, Jesus a supplement of the duties an charities we owe to others."[6] However, the Christian Ethics which Jefferson felt suited man's social nature and contributed to America's virtuous republic, were often lost, in his opinion, in the elaborate ceremonies, dogmas, and institutions of the various churches. Pride and nationalism had often infected the simple, loving teachings of Jesus, distorting Christianity to the world. The violence of The Crusades distorted Jesus' teachings of love, and harmed the spread of God's Truth.

While extolling the ethical teachings of Christ, Jefferson distinguished between the "genuine" lessons of Jesus and the "spurious" dogmas of various sectarian orders. To separate the true teachings of Christ from their imitations (which Jefferson considered as easily distinguishable as "the gold from the dross," the "grain from the chaff," or "as diamonds in a dunghill"),[7] he composed a *Philosophy of Jesus* and a *Life and Morals of Jesus*, by extracting those portions of the Bible which presented the ethics in their purest form.[8] Ironically, it was his abiding and reverent belief in these Christian ethical teachings that led Jefferson to criticize the institutionalized church, and which led many to question his religious sincerity. His attacks on the church and clergy (especially the established Anglican church of Virginia in which he was baptized and served as vestryman) reveal his love of Christian principles. Jefferson chastised the church and Christians for not living up to their divine mission, for not upholding the purity of the Christian faith in a corrupt world. He attacked the church for neglecting its duties, for its hypocrisy and greed in serving worldly authorities rather than measuring them against the high standards of Christian faith and by preaching poverty, peace, charity, and humility while practicing extravagance, persecution, and self-righteous pride.[9] Jefferson's main criticism of the Church was that its distortions of Christ's ethical teachings, essential to a virtuous republic, drove good people away from Jesus' truth and God's love through Christ:

> They are mere usurpers of the Christian name, teaching a counter-religion made up of the *deliria* of crazy imaginations.... Their blasphemies have driven thinking men into infidelity, who have too hastily rejected the supposed author himself, with the horrors so falsely imputed to him. Had the doctrines of Jesus been preached always as pure as they came from his lips, the whole civilized world would now have been Christian.[10]

He hoped people would not judge Jesus by bad "Christians," but by the words of the Bible.

Jefferson's remedy for the perversion of true Christian teaching was the establishment of absolute religious freedom in America, which would spread the teachings of the Bible.

Freedom of Religion and Christian Ethics

Religious freedom and toleration would, for Jefferson, serve the higher purpose of encouraging debate and dialogue among the various religious denominations, from which the simple ethical teaching of Christ, vital to Jefferson's vision of a virtuous republic, might be distilled and disseminated. He hoped that through freedom of religious practice and discussion that those basic teachings of Christ common to all denominations would gain ascendancy, bringing all religious people together and promoting peace and justice in the American republic.[11] In his first inaugural address, Jefferson expressed this, describing the country as "enlightened by a benign religion, professed, indeed, and practiced in various forms, yet all of them including honesty, truth, temperance, gratitude, and the love of man; acknowledging and adoring an overruling Providence."[12] God's plan in history was to bring all people to Christ through the example of Jesus' virtues of love and forgiveness.

Thus, quite the contrary of emanating from a hostility or indifference toward Christianity, Jefferson's advocacy of religious freedom was designed to preserve true Christian teachings from the corruption of worldly institutions: "Had not the Roman government permitted free inquiry Christianity could never have been introduced. Had not free inquiry been indulged at the era of the reformation, the corruptions of Christianity could not have been purged away. If it be restrained now, the present corruptions will be protected, and new ones encourages."[13]

Jefferson's "Bill for Establishing Religious Freedom" began this process of cleansing the Church by denouncing the established Anglican Church for "impiously" obstructing the Christian faith:

> Almighty God hath created the mind free...all attempts to influence it by temporal punishments, or burthens, or by civil incapacitations, tend only to beget habits of hypocrisy and meanness, and are a departure from the plan of the holy author of our religion....[T]he impious presumption of legislature and ruler, civil as well as ecclesiastical...[to] have assumed dominion over the faith of others...tends also to corrupt the principle of that very religion it is meant to encourage.[14]

However, the abolishment of the state church did not, for Jefferson, result in complete religious freedom (by which he meant the exposure to various beliefs and creeds, from which the true, simple teachings of Jesus might be distilled). So, for example, Jefferson opposed the establishment of a Professor of Divinity at the University of Virginia not because a desire to exclude religion from a public institution, but because a *single* Chair of Divinity would imply a single denomination (just as had the established church): "It was not, however, to be understood that instruction in religious opinion and duties was meant to be precluded by the public authorities, as indifferent to the interests of society. On the contrary, the relations which exist between man and his Maker, and the duties resulting from those relations, are the most interesting and important to every human being, and the most incumbent on his study and investigation" (957). Humans must study religion thoroughly to please God.

Jefferson's solution to the problem of one dominant religious group in the public university was not to exclude all religion from the institution, but to invite the free expression of *all* denominations within the university's walls.

> A remedy...has been suggested of promising aspect, which, while it excludes the public authorities from the domain of religious freedom, will give to the sectarian schools of divinity the full benefit the public provisions made for instruction in the other branches of science.... It has, therefore, been in contemplation, and suggested by some pious individuals, who perceive the advantages of associating other studies with those of religion, to establish their religious schools on the confines of the University, so as to give their students ready and convenient access and attendance on the scientific lectures of the University.... Such establishments would offer

> the further and greater advantage of enabling the students of the University to attend religious exercises with the professor of their particular sect, either in the rooms of the building still to be erected...or in the lecturing room of such professor.... Such an arrangement would complete the circle of useful sciences embraced by this institution, and would fill the chasm now existing, on principles which would leave inviolate the constitutional freedom of religion (957–958).

The presence of *all* religious groups within the walls of the public university would give students an opportunity to be exposed to all dogmas, from which, Jefferson hoped, they might distill that which was common to them all—the basic ethical teachings of Jesus and God—to the benefit of the virtuous American republic. Such freedom promoted true religion.

This understanding of freedom of religion is also revealed in Jefferson's description of religious life in Charlottesville, his hometown, where the absence of church buildings compelled the separate churches to worship together, taking turns conducting services in the public courthouse:

> In our village of Charlottesville there is a good deal of religion, with only a small spice of fanaticism. We have four sects, but without either church or meeting house. The courthouse is the common temple, one Sunday in the month to each. Here Episcopalian and Presbyterian, Methodist and Baptist, meet together, join in hymning their Maker, listen with attention and devotion to each other's preachers and all mix in society with perfect harmony.[15]

Such social harmony was precisely what Jefferson hoped freedom of religion would produce in the American republic, as the diverse expression of religious belief distilled the simple ethical teachings of Jesus, fostering love, cooperation, mutual respect, and toleration.[16]

This would free religion from domination by the state, which invariably corrupted it, and from any particular nationality (like the Church of England or the Greek Orthodox Church) which narrowed the universal calling of God through Jesus Christ. The spread of God's truth and mercy would be furthered by religious freedom and individual liberty of conscience. Many religious groups (notably the Baptists) welcomed Jefferson's reforms, which ultimately were enshrined in the First Amendment of the United States Constitution, guaranteeing religious freedom.

Atatürk

Like Jefferson, Kemal Atatürk believed in the absolute individual freedom to believe, express, and communicate religious faith. Only the individual conscience voluntarily can believe in God in a way pleasing to God. As Atatürk said in 1925: "Every individual has the rights and freedoms to think what he wants...to undertake or not undertake, the requirements of the religion he has chosen. No one's ideas or conscience can be dominated."[17] Echoing the Prophet Mohammed in the *Holy Qaran*, "Religion cannot be coerced," Atatürk knew that God is only pleased by free, voluntary submission to His will. Any forced belief is not true faith. To choose one's faith carefully he or she must be free to examine all religions and prayerfully seek God's truth in them. In addition, if in true conscience an individual chooses to be of one faith, no matter which it is (Jewish, Christian, or Moslem), other people and the society must honor God by respecting that choice. The state cannot force a certain religion on the individual nor should it have legal penalties for believing in any faith. Individuals and groups can use only Godly methods of teaching religion: teaching, rational persuasion, and prayer. Not threats, violence, or coercion. Only a faith arrived at freely in true conscience to God is valid and pleasing to God. After that, others should respect that individual decision.

Atatürk's principle of religious freedom is displayed in Turkey's latest (1995) Constitution which reads:

> In line with the concept of nationalism outlined and the reforms and principles introduced by the founder of the Republic of Turkey, Atatürk ...there shall be no interference whatsoever of the sacred religious feelings in State affairs and.... Everyone has the right to life and the right to protect and develop his material and spiritual entity.... Everyone has the right to freedom of conscience, religious belief and conviction. Acts of worship, religious services and ceremonies shall be conducted freely.... No one shall be compelled to worship, or to participate in religious ceremonies and rites, to reveal religious beliefs...or be blamed or accused because of his religious beliefs and convictions.[18]

The Constitution further protects expressing or evangelizing religious beliefs: "Everyone has the right to express and disseminate his thoughts and opinions by speech, in writing, or in pictures or through other media...the freedom to receive and impart information and ideas without interference from official authorities" (14–15). If an individual adult comes to believe, through serious spiritual searching that another religion is true, he or she can convert to that other faith without fear of state or social persecution or punishment. True religion will only flourish and develop in such a free, safe environment. Every man or woman has a right to share that new religious faith.

The first step to achieving the true religious freedom, for Atatürk, was to separate religion from the state. Like Jefferson, he saw that any official enforced state religion, Moslem or Christian, violated individual religious conscience and belief, and dishonored God who gave man free will and wants only freely arrived at faith and voluntary submission to His will. Any state religion that compels belief violates individual belief and dishonors God. So, the historic state religion in Turkey, Islam, represented by the Caliphate, had to be freed from political domination; as Atatürk put it: "It has now become a plainly evident truth that it is necessary to liberate and to elevate the Islamic religion…from its position of being a tool of politics…in order to secure the revival of the Islamic Faith, religion must cease to be a political instrument."[19] Anything less than absolute religious freedom will not please God.

Like the state Anglican Church in Jefferson's Virginia that oppressed religious minorities and violated the true spirit of Christ (love, forgiveness, forbearance), the state-supported Caliphate restricted true religious faith. So, in March 1924, the Grand National Assembly abolished the Islamic Caliphate, or State religion, and freed individual Turkish belief in religion. Faith in God in Turkey has not suffered from this freedom of conscience but has flourished, and like the religious diversity of the Ottoman Empire, which tolerated many religious creeds, modern Turkey is becoming more diverse as it respects individual belief, whether Moslem, Christian, or Jewish. A diversity of Christians is emerging in Turkey, whether Protestant, Catholic, or Orthodox, no longer associated with a certain national or ethnic identity. True faith, as Atatürk understood it, was identified with God, not a certain ethnic group or nationality. The importance was the God-made individual and his or her true seeking after God, whether that searching led to Islam, Christ, or any other religious faith. God would bless the country that permitted free seeking after divine truth and honest choice. At the Friday prayers in Istanbul after the abolition of the Caliphate it was read "Oh God, grant thy protecting aid to our Republican Government…" (386).

Soon after the end of a state religion, Turkey disbanded the Ministry of Religious Affairs, ended the historic office of the Sheikh of Islam, the revenues of the Pious Foundations were confiscated, religious schools were transferred to the secular educational institutions and civil law was put under a Swiss model rather than Islamic Law (386). A Western secular law including the Christian Sunday Sabbath, or Lord's Day, was instituted in Turkey.

The Turkish people accepted these religious reforms inaugurated by Atatürk. Like Jefferson, he was accused by some of being anti-religious, but most Turks recognized that freedom of belief would enhance true religion, not destroy it. Like Christianity in Jefferson's America, religious faith in Turkey is flourishing and healthy. Just as spiritual liberty in the United States has promoted morality there, religious freedom in Turkey will produced greater morality, individual and social.

Atatürk recognized, as Jefferson did, that each individual alone will have to answer to God for his or her faith, so each individual alone must seek and find that faith, whatever it is.

Notes

1. See Garrett Ward Sheldon, *What Would Jefferson Say*? (New York: Penguin 1998), 25–35.
2. Jefferson to John Adams, May 5, 1817, *The Adams-Jefferson Letters*, 2 vols., ed. Lester J. Cappon (Chapel Hill: University of North Carolina Press, 1959), 2:512. See also Eugene R. Sheridan's introduction to Dickenson Ward Adams, ed., *Jefferson's Extracts from the Gospels* (Princeton: Princeton University Press, 1983); William D. Gould, "Religious Opinions of Thomas Jefferson," *Mississippi Valley Historical Review* 20 (September 1933); George M. Knoles, "Religious Ideas of Thomas Jefferson," *Mississippi Valley Historical Review* 30 (September 1943); J. Leslie Hall, "The Religious Opinions of Thomas Jefferson:," *Sewannee Review* 12 (April 1913); Charles B. Sanford, *The Religious Life of Thomas Jefferson* (Charlottesville: University Press of Virginia, 1984); Henry Wilder Foote, *The Religion of Thomas Jefferson* (Boston: Beacon Press, 1960).
3. So, Jefferson's criticism of the ancient moral philosophers was: "In developing our duties to others, they were short and defective. They embraced, indeed, the circles of kindred and friends, and inculcated patriotism, or the love of our county in the aggregate, as a primary obligation; towards our neighbors and countrymen they taught justice, but scarcely viewed them as within the circle of benevolence. Still less have they inculcated peace, charity, and love of our fellow-men, or embraced with benevolence the whole family of mankind" (Jefferson to Dr. Benjamin Rush, April 21, 1803, *The Complete Jefferson*, 948).

   John Diggins notes ironically that Jefferson took the relation of Christian ethics to politics much more seriously than his more orthodox brethren (such as John Adams); see Diggins, *The Lost Soul of American Politics* (New York: Basic Books, 1984), 79.
4. Jefferson to Dr. Benjamin Rush, April 21, 1803, *The Complete Jefferson*, 949.
5. Jefferson to John Adams, October 12, 1813, *A-JL*, 2:384.
6. Jefferson to William short, October 31, 1819, *WTJ*, 15:220.
7. Quoted in Koch, *The Philosophy of Thomas Jefferson*, 23.
8. See Adams, *Jefferson's Extracts from the Gospels*.
9. See Jefferson to John Adams, May 5, 1817, *A-JL*, 2:512; to Wendover, March 13, 1815, *CJ*, 953–55, and to Dr. Benjamin Waterhouse, June 26, 1822, 956.
10. Jefferson to Dr. Benjamin Waterhouse, ibid. See also Jefferson to John Adams, May 5, 1817, ibid.' and to Peter Carr, August 10, 1787, *WTJ*, 6:258–59.
11. Sheldon, 31.
12. Jefferson, "First Inaugural Address," *The Complete Jefferson*, 385.
13. From Jefferson's *Notes on the State of Virginia, The Complete Jefferson*, 675.
14. Jefferson, Bill for Establishing Religious Freedom, *The Complete Jefferson*, 946. It was in relation to an established state church that Jefferson made his famous reference to the "wall of separation" between church and state to the Connecticut Baptists (thought even there he wishes for religious freedom to encourage citizens' "social duties," i.e., knowledge of Christian ethics):

I contemplate with sovereign reverence that act of the whole American people which declared that their legislature should "make no law respecting an establishment of religion, or prohibit the free exercise thereof," thus building a wall of separation between church and state. Adhering to this expression of the supreme will of the nation in behalf of the rights of conscience, I shall see with sincere satisfaction the progress of those sentiments which tend to restore to man all his natural rights, convinced he has no natural right in opposition to his social duties. (Letter to A Committee of the Danbury Baptist Association, January 1, 1802, *The Complete Jefferson*, 518–19).

15. Jefferson to Dr. Thomas Cooper, November, 2, 1822, *WTJ*, 15:404, quoted in Foote, *The Religion of Thomas Jefferson,* 7–8. Despite this ecumenical sentiment, Jefferson, two years later, contributed to the building of separate houses of worship, showing a decided partiality to his own Episcopal church. His account book of March 8, 1824 reads: "I have subscribed to the building of an Episcopal church, two hundred dollars; a Presbyterian church, sixty dollars; and a Baptists, twenty-five dollars," 8.
16. Jefferson's general appreciation of the relation between ethics and politics is revealed in a letter to Judge Augustus B. Woodward (March 24, 1824, *WTJ*, 16:19), in which he states that he regards "ethics, as well as religion, as supplements to law in the government of men"; and to William Johnson (June 1823, *The Complete Jefferson*, 322) that "the state's moral rule of their citizens" will be enhanced by its "enforcing moral duties and restraining vice."
17. Ozal, *Atatürk*, 127.
18. *The Constitution of the Republic of Turkey* (Ankara: Kurtulus 1995), 5, 10, 14.
19. Kinross, 385.

CHAPTER FIVE

PUBLIC EDUCATION

Jefferson

Thomas Jefferson considered free public education important to a democratic republic. "If a nation expects to be ignorant and free: he wrote, "it expects what never was and never will be."[1] Basic education is essential for a people to govern themselves. "Enlighten the people generally and tyranny and oppression of body and mind will vanish like spirits at the dawn of day: (84). Universal, secular public education will have economic, social, and political benefits, for Jefferson. It would give equal opportunity for financial success to everyone of talent and diligence, regardless of their ethnic or economic background. Drawing the most intelligent students into business, law, medicine, military, and government regardless of family or class background would benefit the whole society by not restricting leadership in the professions to a small elite. The brightest, hardest-working students would receive an education all the way through the university, even if they came from a poor family who could not afford it. Thus, a "Natural Aristocracy" of merit would advance to positions of power and prominence to their own benefit and the benefit of the whole society. The general population would become educated enough to wisely elect virtuous, talented, dedicated individuals to positions of governance and protect against political corruption and tyranny. A social equality would be maintained by every citizen attending state schools and learning the same basic history, science, literature, and languages. The content of that public education, for Jefferson, would be classical and secular: the Ancient classics of Western civilization, philosophy, religion, ethics, economics, and Modern history, science, and mathematics. Jefferson himself received such a traditional (albeit private) education in the Judeo-Christian religion; Mediterranean and Roman classics; Ancient and Modern philosophy, languages, law, ethics, economics, science, and math. This thorough education prepared him for a career in law, plantation agriculture, business, and public service. His education informed his Revolutionary arguments and his plans and theories for the new American Republic. His proposal for state education simply provided the same standards of learning for everyone, appropriate to a democracy.

Into his eighteenth-century Virginian society that restricted education to that of private tutors of wealthy children, Jefferson's original motive for establishing ward districts was to provide mass education at public expense. His "Bill for the More General Diffusion of Knowledge" (1779) proposed dividing each county into wards or "hundreds" of sufficient size and population (five to six square miles and one hundred citizens) to support an elementary school. Here the basics of reading, writing, and arithmetic, along with history (ancient and modern) were to be taught to all children, at the public expense, for three years.[2]

The next stage of public education in Jefferson's plan was grammar schools, where Latin, Greek, English, geography, and the higher mathematics would be taught. Each year, "impartial examinations" would be given to children completing their elementary course to determine who, among the "best and most promising genius and disposition" (but too poor to afford it), would proceed to these classical grammar schools at public expense. Out of each county grammar school class, the best student would be selected annually to continue his education for four years longer, free of charge. From among the graduates of this group, the best 50 percent would continue to be supported by the public while attending the university, where "all the useful sciences" (from physics to philosophy, ethics, and economics) would be taught them languages for three years. [3] Thus not all children would go all the way through all the levels of schooling, but enough to prepare them for their work and life.

The real purpose of this public educational system was for society to cultivate each individual's innate capacities, and to thereby promote a more just and harmonious society. "The general objects of this law," he said, "are to provide an education adapted to the years, to the capacity, and to the condition of everyone and directed to their freedom and happiness" by developing the "worth and genius" in the people regardless of "wealth, birth or other accidental condition."[4] It was important for the system to be publicly financed to cultivate "those talents that nature has sown as liberally among the poor as the rich, but which perish without use, if not sought for and cultivated."[5] On this system, Jefferson believed, "the principal foundations of future order will be laid."[6] So, universal public education of that "future order" was not considered by Jefferson to provide only equality of private opportunity, but was designed also to serve the public good. Hence, Jefferson's conception of the public good is not reducible to the sum of private goods, or private ambition. Citizens benefiting from this system owed a patriotic duty to serve and sacrifice for their country.

He noted in his *Commonplace Book* on Montesquieu's *Spirit of the Laws*: "He considers political virtue...as the energetic principle of a democratic republic...and shews that every government should provide that its energetic principle should be the object of the education of its youth."[7] In Jefferson's view, the educational system grounded in ward districts contributed to the public good by (1) educating the populace sufficiently to participate directly in local community affairs and to intelligently select political leaders and representatives; and (2) by providing advanced learning to others capable of receiving it, those possessed of "virtue and wisdom," and who are qualified to being chosen as political leaders and representatives. Thus public education of the whole people was to secure the public happiness of all classes of society.[8] Universal, compulsory, secular public education was best for a republican society. Religious instruction was better taught in the home and church, not the school.

For Jefferson, an "ignorant democracy" was a contradiction in terms ("If a nation expects to be ignorant and free, in a state of civilization, it expects what never was and what never will be");[9] but a society educated in local schools would intelligently participate in its own self-governance: "Every government degenerates when trusted to the rulers.... The people themselves therefore are its only safe depositories. And to render even them safe, their minds must be improved."[10] Universal learning and democracy are inseparable, for Jefferson.

Concurrent with the ward schools' elevation of the masses to a level commensurate with democratic participation, the advanced levels of Jefferson's school system provides students of "wisdom and virtue" with successively more rigorous standards of scholarship to produce a pool of superior minds and morals which the people could select as governors and representatives of a just and happy state.[11] Jefferson clearly explained this intended *political* effect of his educational system in the preamble of his "Bill for the More General Diffusion of Knowledge":

> Whereas it is generally true that people will be happiest whose laws are best, and are best administered, and that laws will be wisely formed, and honestly administered, in proportion as those who form and administer them are wise and honest; whence it becomes expedient for promoting the public happiness that those persons, whom na-

> ture hath endowed with genius and virtue, should be rendered by liberal education worthy to receive and able to guard the sacred deposit of the rights and liberties of their fellow citizens, and that they should be called to that charge without regard to wealth, birth, or other accidental condition or circumstance; but the indigence of the greater number disabling them from so education, at their own expense, those of their children whom nature hath fitly formed and disposed to become useful instruments for the public; it is better that such should be sought for and educated at the common expense of all, than that the happiness of all should be confined to the weak or wicked.[12]

Jefferson's appreciation of public education serving the good of society rather than personal ambition was extended even to his view of teachers. The grammar school teachers were to be selected not only on the basis of their scholarly abilities, but also for their "fidelity to the Commonwealth" and its republican principles.[13] With similar regard for the political side of the teacher's role, Jefferson recommended to the trustees of a Tennessee college the "esteem, respect and gratitude due to those who devote their time and efforts to rendering the youths of every successive age fit *governors* for the next."[14] Of George Wythe's tenure as Professor of Law at William and Mary College, Jefferson wrote: "Wythe's school is numerous. They hold weekly courts.... The professors join in it, and the young men dispute with elegance, method and learning. This single school, by throwing from time to time new hands well-informed into the Legislative, will be of infinite value."[15] He always looked for the *political* benefits of public education.

So, with a concern for qualifying the populace for self-government, cultivating leaders of wisdom and virtue, and seeing teachers as contributing to these political ends, Jefferson found his education system genuinely "public" in every sense. He considered this system, along with the direct democracy of the ward districts, as constituting the "two great measures...without which no republic can maintain itself."[16] He believed that the division of counties into wards for educational purposes would also serve political purposes, providing the geographical boundaries for small, local, participatory democracies: "My partiality for that division is not founded in views of education solely, but infinitely more as the means of a better administration of our government, and the eternal preservation of its republican principles."[17]

For Thomas Jefferson, as for Atatürk later, free public education was essential to a civilized rational republic of progress, equality and economic prosperity. It emphasized secular subjects not because it was anti-religion but because Jefferson felt religion was best taught in the family and church. Spiritual faith tended to be trivialized and distorted if taught in public schools. So, "secularization" meant not against religious truth but separating it from scientific and purely political matters. A religious moral people are necessary to an ethical, healthy republic, but faith is best inculcated at home and church rather than school.

Atatürk

The national public education system that Kemal Atatürk inaugurated in Turkey was to serve essentially the same purposes that Jefferson's plan for public schooling did: universal free education emphasizing rational, secular, scientific subjects to prepare the average citizen for democratic self-government; to prepare the most intellectually gifted for leadership positions in Turkish society (and around the world); and to promote social and economic progress.

To accomplish these educational goals, however, a fundamental change had to occur in the Turkish language and alphabet: it had to be changed from the Arabic script to the Western, Latin alphabet. Attempts to move Turkey from the Middle Eastern Arabic language to the spoken Turkish had been attempted for almost a hundred years, but the Islamic establishment (founded on the Arab *Qaran*) resisted these changes.[18] Written Arabic did not fit the spoken Turkish dialect, so written works were shut off to most Turks, rendering the mass of the population illiterate (441).

In 1928, amidst massive government resistance, Atatürk began this major transition by appointing an Alphabet Commission. Despite opposition, Atatürk forced through the new Turkish alphabet in six weeks. He introduced it at a People's Party festival with the words: "We must free ourselves from these incomprehensible signs that for centuries have held our minds in an iron vice...for a nation to consist of ten to twenty percent of literates and eighty or ninety percent illiterates is shameful . . .. Our nation will show, with its script and with its mind, that its place is with the civilized world" (443). Atatürk knew, what research has since confirmed, that the language a people speak and write affects the way they think, and Western Latin script promoted modern, scientific, rational, progressive, democratic thought.

Atatürk implemented this radical reform forcefully, knowing that on behalf of tradition resistance would be strong. Newspapers were to be using the new Turkish script in three months, schools in the New Year (443). An official remarked, "Today the whole country has been transformed into a classroom, and the headmaster…is [Atatürk] himself. The Turkish people are going to work hard until they pass the exam of that school" (444). In November 1928, the new Western script (cleverly termed "Turkish" rather than Latin" was made law, announced in the National Assembly as to "enable the people of Turkey to read and write [and therefore, think] easily" (444). Quickly millions (especially children) learned the new Turkish language in Latin script. Writing and speaking conformed to one another, and knowledge advanced (444). Turkish civilization entered the Western world of reason and knowledge.

Notes

1. Quoted in *What Would Jefferson Say*? by Garrett Ward Sheldon (New York: Penguin, 1998), 84.
2. In *The Complete Jefferson*, 1049, 1065; see also Jefferson, *Notes on the State of Virginia*, 667–68.
3. *The Complete Jefferson*, 1052–54, 667, 1065. Cf. Plato's rigorous and impartial educational process in *The Republic*, book 3, 413d–414a, book 4, 419a, book 6, 487a. For more on Jefferson's proposed educational system, see letter to Peter Carr, September 7, 1814, *The Complete Jefferson*, 1065; to John Adams, Oct. 28, 1813, *A-JL*, 2:389; and to Governor John Tyler, *WTJ*, 12: 393.

   For white women, Jefferson recommended training in "dancing, drawing and music," as these would enhance their gracefulness and contribute to their domestic charms (see letter to N. Burwell, 1818, *WTJ, 7: 101).*
4. Jefferson, *Notes on the State of Virginia*, 667.
5. Thomas Jefferson, Bill for the More General Diffusion of Knowledge, *The Complete Jefferson*, 1048. Thus, Jefferson's belief in the equal distribution of virtue and talents among all classes of children did not imply the absolute equality of those qualities of every child; Jefferson may not have spoken of intrinsic differences in individual capacities (or of the possibility of gifted parents producing undistinguished offspring and vice-versa) in Plato's terms ("The Myth of the Metals") but he did divide society, for educational purposes, into classes of "laboring and learned," which were both presumably natural and discerned and developed through a discriminating educational system; see Jefferson to Peter Carr, September 7, 1814, *The Complete Jefferson*; Plato's *Republic*, book 3, 415a-d.
6. Jefferson, *Notes on the State of Virginia, The Complete Jefferson*, 667. This does not mean that such a virtue, served by public education, was incompatible, for Jefferson, with economic advancement (see Joyce Appleby, *Capitalism and a New Social Order* [New York: New York University Press, 1984], 14–15).
7. Jefferson, *Commonplace Book*, 259. The relevant passages from Montesquieu, *Spirit of the Laws*, trans. Thomas Nugent (New York: Hafner Press, 1975), 1:33–34, follow:

   > It is in a republican government that the whole power of education is required. The fear of despotic governments naturally arises of itself amidst threats and punishments; the honor of monarchies is favored by the passions, and favors them in its turn; but virtue is a self-renunciation, which is ever arduous and painful.
   >
   > This virtue may be defined as the love of the laws and of our country. As such love requires a constant preference of public to private interest, it is the source of all private virtues; for they are nothing more than this very preference itself.
   >
   > This love is peculiar to democracies. In these alone the government is intrusted to private citizens. Now, a government is like everything else: to preserve it we must love it.

See also David W. Carrithers, "Montesquieu, Jefferson and the Fundamentals of Eighteenth-Century Republican Theory," *The French-American Review* 4 (fall 1982).

8. Cf. Plato's particularized education serving the universal good: "in founding the city we are not looking to the exceptional happiness of any one group among us, but, as far as possible, that of the city as a whole" (*The Republic*, book 4, 420b). I am not suggesting that Jefferson got this idea from what he called "the whimsies, puerilities, and unintelligible jargon" of Plato's *Republic* (letter to John Adams, 1814, *WTJ*, 6:354), only that there appear to be some similarities in their conceptions of education.
9. Jefferson letter to Charles Yancey, *WJT*, 6:517.
10. Jefferson, *Notes on the State of Virginia*, 668; see also Jefferson, Bill for the More General Diffusion of Knowledge, 1048; and Jefferson's letter to Monsieur A. Coray in which he encourages French leaders to elevate the masses by "improving their minds and qualifying them for self-government" (October 31, 1823, *WJT*, 15: 481).
11. Jefferson's emphasis on a public dimension of happiness in what follows reveals his classical republican bent, as opposed to the purely private, individualistic "happiness" of liberalism, and gives clues to his substitution of "happiness" for "property" in the Declaration of Independence. Wood, *The Creation of the American Republic*, 72–75, discusses the place of education in republican ideology.
12. Cf. James Harrington's educational system (*Oceana*, ed. S. B. Liljegreen [Westport, Conn.: Hyperion Press, 1979], 168: "And the formation of a Citizen in the Womb of the Common-wealth is his Education. That which is proposed for the erecting and endowing of Schools throughout the Tribes capable of all the Children of the same, and able to give unto the Poor the Education of theirs *Gratis*, is only matter of direction in the case of very great Charity, as easing the needy of they Charge of their Children from the ninth to the fifteenth year of their Age."
13. Jefferson, Bill for the More General Diffusion of Knowledge, 1052.
14. Jefferson to Hugh L. White et al., May 6, 1810, *WTJ*, 12:388 (emphasis mine).
15. Jefferson to James Madison, 1780, *WTJ* (Ford ed.), 2:322.
16. Jefferson to Gov. John Tyler, May 26, 1810, *WTJ* (mem. ed.), 12:393; see also Jefferson to Joseph C. Cabell, Jan. e1, 1914, *WTJ*, 14:84 ("There are two objects, indeed, which I shall claim a right to further as long as I breath, the public education, and the substitution of counties into wards. I consider the continuance of republican government as absolutely hanging on these two hooks").
17. Jefferson to Gov. Wilson C. Nicholes, April 2, 1816, *WTJ*, 14:454; and as Jefferson wrote to Joseph C. Cabell of the wards (February 2, 1816, 423): "Begin them only for a single purpose; they will soon show for what others they are the best instruments."
18. Kinross, *Atatürk*, 441.

CHAPTER SIX

ECONOMICS

Jefferson

A democratic economics system was essential to the American Republic for Jefferson. He saw the old monopolistic imperial system, which concentrated wealth in a few politically prominent people incompatible with democratic equality. For a republic to be real, economic activity and wealth must be widely distributed amongst the people. Without economic independence, political rights are a fiction; without a large middle-class citizenry, politics will be controlled by a small minority of rich people who corrupt the government. Hence, Jefferson, like Atatürk after him, encouraged laws that distributed land and property across the masses of common people, making them politically independent and incorruptible. Similarly, he endorsed a graduated income tax which took more money from the very wealthy citizens and distributed it to the very poorest, needy people.

One of the wealthiest men in Virginia, Jefferson owned over ten thousand acres of land and two hundred slaves. He built a large mansion (Monticello) and operated several small manufacturing operations on his plantation. Like Atatürk's experimental model farm, Jefferson employed modern agricultural techniques and implements, seeking to make the American economy more independent and productive.[1] He invented a new plow and borrowed many new inventions from Europe. Ironically, he died bankrupt and lost the family home to creditors. This was partly because he spent money extravagantly, he underwrote various friends' debts who defaulted on their loans leaving him owning the debts, and a general depression of the Virginia economy in the early 1800s. Jefferson bought thousands of books (which eventually formed the original Library of Congress); in London he purchased boots, gloves, hats, a harness, maps, pistols, pocketbooks, scientific equipment, tools, clothes, shoes, slippers and a harpsichord. He, like Kemal Atatürk later, was as generous a giver as he was extravagant a getter. He sent his friends books and equipment he knew they would enjoy and showered gifts on his family members (especially girls) of dresses, saddles, books, Bibles, musical instruments, furniture, games, and horses. However, he never forgot the essentially public and political nature of economics and property.

Jefferson's emphasis upon economic independence as requisite to a democratic citizenry and his criticism of economic manipulation by politicians (public credit, stockjobbing, financial imperialism) place him within the classical republican camp, but his affinity for certain kinds of economic development and free market commerce make him in favor of capitalism—but a capitalism regulated by the state. When we find that Jefferson saw economics contributing to independent citizens and an independent nation, he approved of them; and where he saw economic policies detracting from an independent, educated, and politically active citizenry and self-sufficient republic, he opposed them.

Jefferson made several economic reforms in Virginia shortly after returning from Philadelphia essential to his conception of ward democracy. These economic policies supported Jefferson's educational and political structures by providing the material self-sufficiency and independence for the community of citizens to develop their social faculties and participate in self-government. Jefferson's Virginia reforms accomplished this by eliminating the oligarchy of concentrated wealth along with its exclusive hold on politics and elevating the mass of citizens to economic independence, making them capable and interested in public participation.[2]

Jefferson hoped to bring down the oligarchy of concentrated wealth in Virginia by abolishing the laws of primogeniture and entail. Both primogeniture (which preserved large estates by restricting inheritance to the eldest son) and entail (which prohibited the division and sale of estates) dated from a time when the feudal nobility tried to protect itself from the rising monied classes. Jefferson, like those new classes that strove to break up the old aristocracy hoped to dissolve the Virginia oligarchy's preeminent control over the land and its corresponding monopoly over public affairs.[3] Unlike other critics of the landed nobility who wished simply to eliminate the oligarchy's predominant position by transferring its power and wealth to themselves, Jefferson proposed redistributing that landed property and influence among the population generally, providing the people with an economic independence commensurate with respectable participation in the life of the republic.

Atatürk's redistribution of land to Turkish farmers followed the same logic.

In his "Proposed Constitution for Virginia" (1776), Jefferson included a provision for establishing relative economic equality: "Every person of full age neither owning nor having owned [50] acres of land, shall be entitled to an appropriation of [50] acres or so much as shall make up what he owns or has owned [50] acres in full and absolute dominion."[4] So, Jefferson believed that because political power followed property ownership, a virtuous republic must have an economically independent citizenry and general equality of condition in moderate wealth.[5] Hence, in his *Commonplace Book*, Jefferson noted Montesquieu's dictum: "In a democracy, equality and frugality should be promoted by the laws…by laying burthens on the richer classes and encouraging the poorer ones."[6]

This is why Jefferson was so shocked at the extremes of wealth and poverty in prerevolutionary France, as he detailed in a letter to James Madison (October 28, 1785) after giving money to a beggar woman:

> She burst into tears of a gratitude which I could perceive was unfeigned…
>
> This little *attendrissement*, with the solitude of my walk led me into a train of reflections of that unequal division of property which occasions the numberless instances of wretchedness which I had observed in this country and is to be observed all over Europe. The property of this country is absolutely concentrated in a very few hands, having revenues of from half a million of guineas a year downwards….
>
> I asked myself what could be the reason that so many should be permitted to beg who are willing to work, in a country where there is a very considerable proportion of uncultivated lands? These lands are kept idle mostly for the sake of game….
>
> I am conscious that an equal division of property is impracticable. But the consequences of this enormous inequality producing so much misery to the bulk of mankind, legislators cannot invent too many devices for subdividing property, only taking care to let their subdivisions go hand in hand with the natural affections of the human mind…
>
> Another means of silently lessening the inequality of property is to exempt all from taxation below a certain point, and to tax the higher portions of property in geometrical progression as they rise. Whenever there is in any country uncultivated lands and unemployed poor, it is clear that the laws of property have been so far extended as to violate natural right. The earth is given as a common stock for man to labour and live on. If, for the encouragement of industry we allow it to be appropriated, we must take care that other employment be furnished to those excluded from the appropriation. If we do not the fundamental right to labour the earth returns to the unemployed. It is too soon yet in our country to say that every man who cannot find employment but who can find uncultivated land, shall be a liberty to cultivate it, paying a moderate rent. But it is not too soon to provide by every possible means

> that as few a possible shall be without a little portion of land. The small landholders are the most precious part of a state.[7]

Jefferson's view that farmers are "the most precious part of a state" is well known. It is the landowner's economic independence that produces his public virtue and qualifies him for political participation, for Jefferson.

> Those who labour in the earth are the chosen people of God, if ever he had a chosen people, whose breasts he has made his peculiar deposit for substantial and genuine virtue. It is the focus in which he keeps alive that sacred fire, which otherwise might escape from the face of the earth. Corruption of morals in the mass of cultivators is a phenomenon of which no age nor nation has furnished an example. It is the mark set on those, who not looking up to heaven, to their own soil and industry, as does the husbandman, for their subsistence, depend for it on the casualties and caprice of customers. Dependence begets subservience and venality, suffocates the germ of virtue, and prepares fit tools for the designs of ambition.[8]

Jefferson even encouraged Virginia farmers to plant wheat instead of tobacco because it was easier to grow and would allow greater leisure for public participation and virtue.[9]

His hatred for the "mobs of the cities" was not due to a purely anti-urban bias (he loved Paris), but rather that the "ignorance, poverty and vice" of city dwellers disqualified them for wise, independent, and virtuous political participation.[10] Power in the hands of European city mobs, Jefferson wrote to Adams, "would be instantly perverted to the demolition and destruction of everything public and private."[11] When later in his life Jefferson modified his agrarian ideal to accommodate domestic cities and manufacturers, it was again to secure economic independence—this time for the nation:

> We must now place the manufacturer by the side of the agriculturist.... Shall we make our own comforts, or go without them, at the will of a foreign nation? He, therefore, who is against domestic manufacture must be for reducing us either to dependence on that foreign nation or to be clothed in skins, and to live, like wild beasts, in dens...I am not one of these; experience has taught me that manufacturers are now as necessary to our independence as to our comfort."[12]

Jefferson's late appreciation of "a due balance between agriculture, manufactures and commerce,"[13] producing national independence, now required a citizen with economic independence either in land ownership or a "satisfactory situation," to maintain a qualified democratic citizenry and a democratic republic. As he wrote to John Adams in 1813: "Everyone, by his property, or by his satisfactory situation, is interested in the support of law and order. And such men may safely and advantageously reserve to themselves a wholesome control over their public affairs."[14] For those without land or skills, Jefferson proposed a "workforce" style of government assistance, retraining, and public works.

So, Jefferson's criticism of Hamilton and the Federalists' policies, centered around their corruption of this classical republican balance, by concentrating political power in the central government (as opposed to the states and localities) and concentrating economic power in the hands of a few wealthy merchants and bankers (through policies of paper money, public credit, and so forth). For Jefferson, as for other classical republican thinkers, there was a constant struggle between a corrupt centralized government that wished to control all wealth and power (giving it out as patronage to control the masses) and a strong, independent, democratic citizenry capable of ruling itself with wisdom, virtue, and self-respect. His idea of economically independent, publicly educated, and politically experienced citizens that would be capable of self-governance and strong enough to resist the manipulations and encroachments of a Federalist administration formed his democratic economics.

In the end, Jefferson saw economically independent citizens able to rule themselves honestly and prosperously. Capitalism, private property, and representative government go together, just as centralized government power and economic monopoly and corruption go hand-in-hand. A republic may use the law to maintain a strong, independent, educated middle class; but to do so it must resist the temptation (that Jefferson saw in the Federalists) to concentrate power and money in the central regime. Corruption by the few would lead to poverty for the many if politicians were not disciplined and honest, as Atatürk was. It forms a constant struggle to use political power wisely and fairly, while not "feathering one's nest" with public funds, so easily done by those in political power. Without respect for the common people's prosperity, politics easily become a game for accumulating personal wealth. Ultimately, patriotism and love of country only can overcome greed and corruption.

Atatürk

Like Jefferson, Atatürk believed that a true Republic requires an economically independent and prosperous citizenry. Mass poverty and concentrated wealth in a corrupt political elite is not consistent with a healthy, democratic society. So, as with Jefferson's economic reforms in Virginia, Atatürk sought to reform the Turkish economy to promote prosperity and broad distribution of wealth. Either through land ownership or satisfactory employment, Turkey, like America, was to be a predominantly middle-class country. Living in the industrialized twentieth century, Atatürk used some different means from Jefferson to accomplish this end, but the ultimate goal of individual and national economic self-sufficiency and independence was the same.[15]

Atatürk shared Thomas Jefferson's love of the countryside and farmland. Since his boyhood he loved to walk in the open air, look at the open spaces and observe growing things in nature (390). Even after assuming the presidency of Turkey, he took frequent refuge on the model farm he developed near his old headquarters at the Agricultural School near Chankaya (just as Jefferson as President frequently retreated to the peace and beauty of his mountain farm, Monticello). The founder of modern Turkey, like the American, had a lifelong interest in agricultural development. He supervised the planting of an orchard at the model farm, which became an experimental station for Turkey's forestry and horticulture. Tapping new sources of water, Atatürk employed modern irrigation to foster the orchards and fields (390). He, like the Virginian, sought agricultural innovations to raise production of basic foodstuffs and saw the farmer as the backbone of the national economy.

Atatürk advanced this agrarian concern with a series of reforms: abolishment of the legal tithes which kept Turkish farmers impoverished and backward; altering systems of land ownership and tenure; redistributing land from the large estates to landless peasants and immigrants (448). These innovations, like Jefferson's encouragement of small yeoman farmer citizens in America, fostered a new class of small Turkish landowners—independent and productive. If Turkey was to develop economically, Atatürk reasoned it must be agriculturally productive enough to feed its growing population and create a surplus to buy other commodities from abroad (448).

However, like Jefferson's economic plan, Atatürk's policies recognized the need for balancing agriculture with industry and commerce.

Although private enterprise was encouraged, the state managed monopoly industries in basic industries and utilities (petroleum, shipping, salt, sugar, matches, tobacco, alcohol, and so forth) (448). Like most modern Western economics, Turkey's became a mixture of private capitalism and public socialism. The key to economic development is in the proper mix. Seeing the early, extensive state ownership of many businesses, one official remarked, "when are we going to have a monopoly of kebab" (448)? Actually most publicly controlled industries were basic: steel, mining, banking, railways, and so on, needed to foster a modern, European economy, but care had to be taken to keep them from destroying free enterprise (449).

The mix of public and private has continued in modern Turkey, as in all Western countries; but the emphasis has shifted periodically. Atatürk's vision of a free, advanced, prosperous economy, premised in agriculture but including industry, banking, and commerce, appropriate to a middle-class Republic, has continued.

Notes

1. See Sheldon, *The Political Philosophy of Thomas Jefferson* (Baltimore: Johns Hopkins University Press, 1991), chapter 4; and *What Would Jefferson Say*? chapter 7.
2. Cf. Aristotle on the relation between politics and economics: "Now property is part of a household and the acquisition of property part of the economics of a household; for neither life itself nor the good life [i.e., *Politics*] is possible without a certain minimum standard of wealth" (*Politics*, book 1, ch. 4, 3).
3. See Jefferson to John Adams, Oct. 28, 1813, *A-JL*, 2:389, 391; Jefferson, The Bill to Abolish Entails (1776), in *The Complete Jefferson*, 88; and Jefferson, *Autobiography*, 50–57.
4. In *Cf*, 109; Jefferson understood the corollary requisite of such property in the strict regulation of immigration (see *Notes on the State of Virginia*, 624–26).
5. Drew McCoy, *The Elusive Republic: The Political Economy in Jeffersonian America* (Chapel Hill: University of North Carolina Press, 1980).
6. Jefferson, *Commonplace Book*, 259. Jefferson, like Aristotle, and unlike Plato, preferred to keep economics a private or "household" matter rather than a purely private (a la Plato's communism) matter; but, recognizing the public implications of private property, Jefferson sought to preserve a rough equality of wealth, very much like Rousseau's famous statement: "By equality, we should understand, not that the degrees of power shall never be great enough for violence; and shall always be exercised by virtue of rank and law; and that, in respect to riches, no citizen shall ever be wealthy enough to buy another, and none poor enough to be forced to sell himself...allow neither rich men nor beggars. These two estates, which are naturally inseparable, are equally fatal to the common good")*The Social Contract*, trans. G. D. H. Cole [New York: Dutton, 1977], 204). Cf. Montesquieu (*Spirit of the Laws* 1:41–42): "The good sense and happiness of individuals depend greatly upon the mediocrity of their abilities and fortunes. Therefore, as a republic, where the laws have placed many in a middling station, is composed of wise men, it will be wisely governed; as it is composed of happy men, it will be extremely happy"; and Harrington (*Oceana*, 17): "You have Aristotle full of it in divers places, especially where he saith that Immoderate Wealth, as where One man or the Few have greater possessions than equality or the frame of the Common-wealth will bear, is an occasion of Sedition, which ends for the greater part in Monarchy; and that for this cause the Ostracisms hath been received in divers places, as in *Argo* and *Athens*. But that it were better to prevent the growth in the beginning, then, when it hath gotten head, to seek the remedy of such an evil." See also Aristotle (*Politics*, book 9, ch. 11, 171–772): "cities have every chance of being well-governed in which the middle class is large, stronger if possible than the other two together, or at any rate stronger than one of them. For the addition of its weight to either side will turn the balance and prevent the extravagances of the opposition. For this reason it is a happy state of affairs when those who take part in the life of the state have a moderate but adequate amount of property."

7. A similar letter to Madison in 1787, when Jefferson was again writing from France, develops his famous "earth belongs to the living" theme again urging the redistribution of landed property every generation through legal means.
8. Jefferson, *Notes on the State of Virginia*, 678. Cf. Aristotle (*Politics*, book 6, ch. 4, 240): "An agricultural population makes the best demos; so that it is in fact possible to make a democracy anywhere where the population subsists in agriculture or stock-raising and pastures"; and Harrington (*Oceana*, 169): "Agriculture is the Bread of the Nation, we are hung upon it by the teeth; it is a mighty Nursery of Strength, the best Army, and the most assured Knapsack; it is managed with the least turbulent or ambitious, and most innocent hands of all other Arts. Wherefore I am of Aristotle's opinion, That a Common-wealth of Husband-men (and such is ours) must be the best of all others."
9. T. H. Breen, "The Culture of Agriculture: The Symbolic World of the Tidewater Planter, 1760–1790," in *Saints and Revolutionaries*, eds. David Hall, John Murrin, and Thad Tate (New York: Norton, 1984), 183–84.
10. Jefferson to John Adams, Oct. 28, 1813, *A-JL*, 2:391. Cf. Aristotle (*Politics*, book 6, ch. 4, 242–43): "Their lives are inferior, and the work they do has not the quality of goodness; they are mere labourers, hirelings, the most ordinary specimens of humanity."
11. Jefferson, *A-JL*. Elsewhere Jefferson contrasted "the rabble" of France with the "steady and rational" citizens of America, again attributing this difference, in part, to their respective economic circumstances (see *The Anas*, in *The Complete Jefferson*, 1213).
12. Jefferson to Benjamin Austin, January, 1816, *WTJ*, 6:521.
13. Jefferson to Thomas Leiper, 1809, *WTJ*, 5:417.
14. Jefferson, *A-JL* 2:391. Cf. Aristotle: "the government of a state is rule over free and equal persons" (*Politics*, book 1, ch. 6, 37); this would have led him to question any socialist politics which reduce all politics merely to reflections of economic activity. The ancients considered the satisfaction of material needs as freeing the individual to participate in community life for its own sake: "[Political] life is action, not production" (*Politics*, book 1, ch. 4); "a state is something more than an investment; its purpose is not merely to provide a living but to make a life that is worthwhile. Otherwise, a state might be made up of slaves or animals, and that is impossible, because slaves and animals are not free agents and do not participate in well-being" (book 3, ch. 9, 119).
15. Kinross, *Atatürk*, 448.

EPILOGUE

PHILOSOPHICAL LEGACIES

Jefferson

On his grave stone, Thomas Jefferson listed three accomplishments that he wanted to be remembered for: (1) writing the Declaration of Independence (which proclaimed the nationhood of the United States of America); (2) writing the Virginia Statute for Religious Freedom (which ended the official state church and allowed free, pure religion to flourish in America); and (3) establishing the University of Virginia (the pinnacle of public education that realized social equality of opportunity in America). Those are Jefferson's main legacies: founding the American republic as an independent democracy; creating a secular government which protected individual rights and encouraged social responsibility and participation, while ensuring religious liberty and purity; building an egalitarian society and culture through a shared educational background and advancement by merit and virtue regardless of past poverty or ignorance. These legacies form the American ethos more than those of any other Founder of America. James Madison more meticulously constructed the United States Constitution; George Washington was more impressive as a military and political leader; but Jefferson's ideals remain the United States of America's basic principles. Professor Merrill Peterson in *The Jeffersonian Image in the American Mind* (Oxford, 1960) says that America's image of itself reflects its view of Jefferson. His ideals reappear again and again in American history: from Jacksonian democracy to Theodore Roosevelt's continental expansion to FDR's New Deal, to President Clinton's disgrace, Jefferson's life and teachings are invoked. He embodies American notions of the equality of all men, the necessity of democracy; the blessing of freedom, the decency of Christian ethics, the reality of selfishness, greed, and evil; and the optimistic hope for a brighter future if people are educated, economically self-sufficient, democratically involved, and spiritually aware. Thomas Jefferson is the "Everyman" in the U.S.A. despite his privilege and wealth, his sexism and racism, his hypocrisy and self-delusion at times; Jefferson and his views form an ideal American "type." Inventive, rational, optimistic, thoughtful, a family man, communicative and, above all, democratic. A Renaissance Man with interests in science, literature, law, architecture, agriculture, education, religion, economics, ethics, and etiquette. A man with many friends, a loving family and an adoring public.[1]

Thomas Jefferson is revered in America, as Atatürk is in modern Turkey, as genius. Self-sacrificing for the public good of his country; noble in attitude and life. Jefferson is used by all political parties and most social movements: liberal and conservative, socialist, capitalist, agricultural, environmentalist, industrial, religious, and scientific, Left and Right. His wisdom enlightens all periods of American history and is spread abroad to Latin American countries seeking independence, Chinese revolutionaries, and modern France, Italy, and Turkey. His cherished ideals of individual freedom: of conscience, speech, press, and religion, as necessary to progress and happiness, remain the cornerstones of his ideology. Without individual liberty, nothing of human value can be accomplished, because God made man with free will: to accept or reject Him, to seek to know Him in His fullness; to choose to follow His ways. So, Jefferson's ideals of freedom, democracy, equality, and rights constitute his real legacy.

Jefferson's concept of freedom encompasses both the liberal, Lockean ideas of individual freedom from government interference and the classical notion of freedom to participate in the public deliberation which develops one's highest qualities and shapes the laws under which one lives. Both ancient and modern conceptions of democracy are reconciled by Jefferson's adaptation of Lockean freedom to serve the ends of classical freedom embodied in local democratic legislatures, and his belief that participatory republics would protect individual natural rights.

Jefferson's earliest and most familiar perception of freedom in the Declaration of Independence, and involves freedom from arbitrary, tyrannical corrupt government defined by Locke's free, equal, and independent individuals possessed of natural rights who must legitimately submit only to limited authority to which they consent. This liberal creed, designed by Locke for use by free and independent individuals in the state of nature, was adapted by Jefferson for free and independent states (first in the colonial legislatures and then in the state democracies) against the arbitrary and corrupt rule of distant, commercial regimes (first in the British Parliament and then in the federal government), leading to freedom to rule democratically.

Jefferson's use of the liberal conception of freedom was altered to mean not just liberty from governmental tyranny over the individual, but liberty from centralized government's usurpation of local, democratic sovereignty. Furthermore, Jefferson's invocation of Lockean freedom on behalf of small democratic republics followed from a nonliberal appreciation of humans which sees that certain of the qualities of classical republics, like their cultivation of virtue through direct participation in community life, cannot be replicated in a large-scale, highly centralized corrupt regime. The fact that Jefferson had faith in a small-scale, participatory republic's ability to protect individual rights and liberties implies that he found the greatest threat to individual rights from remote, corrupt centralized government, not local or state government where citizens are more likely to be actively involved, rendering those governments more responsive and responsible. Jefferson's idea of freedom revolved around participation in a society of which the individual is a natural part. If man is naturally a social being inevitably residing in a political society, true freedom does not consist only in private liberty and detachment from the community, but in the realization of the individual's noblest qualities and submission to the laws he has helped to create.[2]

Jefferson argues for freedom of religion not because he believes that the essential ethical truths of Christianity are invalid or unknowable, but because he regards the free discussion of the various interpretations of Scripture as the most effective means of individually discovering and inculcating those essential religious truths. Jefferson is not the staunchest advocate of the free press merely for the sake of abstract freedom, but because he believed that "freedom of the press...is the best instrument for enlightening the mind of man, and improving him as a rational, moral, and social being."[3] Jeffersonian freedom includes freedom from arbitrary rule and freedom to actively participate in shaping one's social destiny toward the end of more decent, intelligent, and contented citizens.

Jefferson's democracy grew from small ward republics in which citizens regularly participate, along with that system of representation which grows out of local democracy and is characterized by a natural aristocracy of wisdom and virtue. Founded on the assumption that man is naturally a social animal, capable of knowing and preserving the common good. For Jefferson, this classical democracy of the ward republics provided the most efficient administration of public policy by cultivating the citizens' hearts and minds: by developing both their affectionate regard for the community and nation and their rational faculties requisite to wise public deliberation. Jefferson believed society must provide the educational, political, and economic means necessary for such a democracy.

A country consisting of small republics providing political freedom, educational opportunity, and economic equality will more likely produce representatives from the natural aristocracy of wisdom and virtue capable of knowing the common good; while a society lacking such requisites of democracy will more likely be governed by one of the artificial aristocracies of wealth or birth which, at best, is capable of knowing its own private good.

Thus, Jefferson's economically independent, educated, and active democratic citizenry was "virtuous" in both the functional and the moral sense, it was qualified to function as a self-governing body (which is impossible under conditions of economic deprivation or dependence, ignorance, or passivity), and it comes through such self-governance, to see individual benefit in the common good.

Jefferson may have asserted, in that oft-quoted phrase from the Declaration of Independence, that "all men are created equal"; however, his later thought suggests that he believed most men revealed their inequality shortly after that creation. Jefferson regarded men as equal in some ways and unequal in others, but in a just society the inequalities among individuals were neither necessarily degrading nor injurious. Different talents and abilities can blend together to form a social harmony.

Jefferson considered men equal in the liberal sense of possessing common traits in the physical senses, material needs, and powers, and in the rights to self-preservation attending those qualities. However he also considered men equal in the classical sense of being naturally social animals capable of moral choice and just action. Yet it was precisely in this classical definition of man's highest faculties that Jefferson emphasized the unequal distribution of the wisdom and virtue that makes social harmony and justice possible, and resides in a common dependence on one another and a shared devotion to the public good. While a natural aristocracy is superior to ordinary citizens in virtue and wisdom, it also depends on them for its recognition and election positions of public trust.

Jefferson's appreciation of human rights is often associated with Lockean natural rights protecting the individual from governmental incursion into one's life, liberty, and property. Jefferson conceived of such rights as free speech and free press not as ends in themselves, but as necessary parts of a deliberative life of small republics. Without free speech, participatory democracy cannot exist; without participatory democracy, man's social nature remains undeveloped. So, while Lockean rights tend to emphasize man's private interests and economic existence, Jeffersonian rights emphasize man's public nature and political life, serving the common good.

Jefferson's political theory implies those substantive rights necessary to the realization of free speech, free press, and free assembly, that is, rights to an education suited to the individual's capacities, a measure of economic independence, and the opportunity to shape one's social destiny at the local community level. Or, Jefferson's theory implies the right to be free from inadequate education, degrading poverty, corrupt government, and bureaucratic fiat. If man's noblest quality is to be cultivated, and that quality resides in a moral sense enlightened by ethical teachings, another Jeffersonian right might be the opportunity to be exposed to, but not indoctrinated in, a variety of religious perspectives, the individual being free to choose the Truth that God leads them to, regardless of social, cultural, or family pressure.

Jefferson's real legacy, then, is what is best in America: freedom with responsibility; individual rights with a social conscience; fulfillment with a sense of gratitude to one's country and God. That legacy lives on wherever the best in Americans is displayed: compassion, cooperation, and charity. It remains a critical ideal against which to measure current faults and shortcomings, and America is the better for it.

Atatürk

Like Jefferson, Atatürk's legacy was wide-ranging and multifarious. He won his country's independence; he established a modern Western-style republic; he promoted religious freedom and liberty of conscience; he advanced an industrial economy and public education in Turkey; he caused his homeland to receive honor and respect around the world. His new name "Atatürk" meant, appropriately, "Father of the Turks." As Lord Patrick Kinross aptly summarized his accomplishments:

> The Turkey which now existed on the map, a compact whole salvaged from the wide-strewn fragments of the Ottoman Empire, was his creation. But for him it might have been reduced to a mere fragment itself, enclosed by the empires of others and perhaps eventually absorbed as a satellite by one of them. He had made of it a nation, reviving its patriotism and restoring its self-respect. He had given it a dura-

> ble political system. From among its people he was moulding a new type of Turk, fitting him by education and example to rank with the peoples of Europe, releasing him from a dead past to seek a place for his country in contemporary civilization.[4]

Atatürk's legacy, like Jefferson's, is literally transforming his world, from a backward, decadent, corrupt, enslaved society to a modern, democratic, progressive country. Like America, Turkey is still growing towards the ideals of freedom and progress that Atatürk envisioned. Moreover, comparing this lively, advanced country to those around it that didn't benefit from Atatürk's efforts, the magnitude of his accomplishment is apparent. This fact has been recognized by leaders around the world. Just as Jefferson is seen as the "Prophet of Democracy" all over the world, Atatürk has impressed great men with remaking the region of the Near and Middle East. British Prime Minister David Lloyd George wrote: "The centuries rarely produce a genius…that great genius of our era was granted to the Turkish nation."[5] Winston Churchill wrote that "Atatürk's death is not only a loss for the country, but for Europe is the greatest loss…."[6]

The founder of Moslem Pakistan, Muhammed ali Jinnah, said of Atatürk that "He proved with the founding of Turkey that he had the power to make the Moslems' voices heard by all nations in the world" (347). French President Charles de Gaulle wrote that because of Atatürk "Turkish history even more than ever is inseparable from Western and European history" (347). "In the life of a nation it is very seldom that changes to such a radical degree were carried out in such a short period of time…because of this, Turkey can be proud of itself," according to the Greek Prime Minister Eleutherios Venizelos in 1933 (346). For American President and hero of World War II, General Dwight Eisenhower, Atatürk was an "inspiration to free peoples throughout the world" (346). John F. Kennedy, the American President often compared to Thomas Jefferson, said that "The name of Atatürk reminds people of the historical success of…farsightedness in the understanding of the modern world and courage and power as a military leader" (347).

Atatürk's legacy lives on in many ways in modern Turkey, especially where love for country, dedication to the common good, and devotion to individual rights and freedom prevail.

Notes

1. See Sheldon *What Would Jefferson Say*? (New York: Penguin, 1998) esp. Introduction and Chapters 3, 5, and 8.
2. Cf. Rousseau's definition of true liberty as "obedience to a law we prescribe to ourselves," *The Social Contract*, ed. G. D. H. Cole (New York: Dutton, 1973), book 1, ch. 7, 174.
3. Jefferson to Monsieur A. Coray, Oct. 31, 1823, in Jefferson, *The Writings of Thomas Jefferson*, 20 vols., ed. Albert Ellery Bergh (Washington, D.C.: Thomas Jefferson Memorial Assoc., 1904–05), 15:489.
4. Kinross, *Atatürk*, 474.
5. Mehmet Ozel, *Atatürk*, 346.
6. Ozel, *Atatürk*, 346.

APPENDIX I

THE CONSTITUTION OF THE UNITED STATES OF AMERICA

We the People *of the United States, in order to form a more perfect union, establish Justice, insure domestic tranquility, provide for the common defence, promote the general Welfare, and secure the Blessings of Liberty to ourselves and our Posterity, do ordain and establish this Constitution for the United States of America.*

ARTICLE I

SECTION 1. All legislative Powers herein granted shall be vested in a Congress of the United States, which shall consist of a Senate and a House of Representatives.

SECTION 2. The House of Representatives shall be composed of Members chosen every second Year by the People of the several States, and the Electors in each State shall have the Qualifications requisite for Electors of the most numerous Branch of the State Legislature.

No Person shall be a Representative who shall not have attained to the Age of twenty-five Years, and been seven Years a Citizen of the United States, and who shall not, when elected, be an Inhabitant of the State in which he shall be chosen.

Representatives and direct Taxes shall be apportioned among the several States which may be included within this Union, according to their respective Numbers, which shall be determined by adding to the whole Number of free Persons, including those bound to Service for a Term of Years, and excluding Indians not taxed, three fifths of all other Person. The actual Enumeration shall be made within three Years after the first Meeting of the Congress of the United States, and within every subsequent Term of ten Years, in such Manner as they shall by Law direct. The Number of Representatives shall not exceed one for every thirty Thousands, but each State shall have at

Least one Representative; and until such enumeration shall be made, the State of New Hampshire shall be entitled to chuse three, Massachusetts eight, Rhode-Island and Providence Plantations one, Connecticut five, New-York six, New Jersey four, Pennsylvania eight, Delaware one, Maryland six, Virginia ten, North Carolina five, South Carolina five, and Georgia three.

When vacancies happen in the Representation from any State, the Executive Authority thereof shall issue Writs of Election to fill such Vacancies.

The House of Representatives shall chuse their Speaker and other Officers; and shall have the sole Power of Impeachment.

When vacancies happen in the Representation from any State, the Executive Authority thereof shall issue Writs of election to fill such Vacancies.

The House of Representatives shall chuse their Speaker and other Officers; and shall have the sole Power of Impeachment.

SECTION 3. The Senate of the United States shall be composed of two Senators from each State, chosen by the Legislature thereof, for six Years; and each Senator shall have one Vote.

Immediately after they shall be assembled in Consequence of the first Election, they shall be divided as equally as may be into three Classes. The Seats of the Senators of the first Class shall be vacated at the Expiration of the second Year, of the second Class at the Expiration of the fourth Year, and of the third Class at the Expiration of the sixth Year, so that one-third may be chosen every second Year; and if Vacancies happen by Resignation, or otherwise, during the Recess of the Legislature of any State, the Executive thereof may make temporary Appointments until the next Meeting of the Legislature, which shall then fill such Vacancies.

No Person shall be a Senator who shall not have attained to the Age of thirty Years, and been nine Years a Citizen of the United States, and who shall not, when elected, be an Inhabitant of that State for which he shall be chosen.

The Vice President of the United States shall be President of the Senate, but shall have no Vote, unless they be equally divided.

The Senate shall chuse their other Officers, and also a President pro tempore, in the Absence of the Vice President, or when he shall exercise the Office of President of the United States.

The Senate shall have the sole Power to try all Impeachments. When sitting for that Purpose, they shall be on Oath or Affirmation. When the President of the United States is tried, the Chief Justice shall preside: And no Person shall be convicted without the Concurrence of two-thirds of the Members present.

Judgment in Cases of Impeachment shall not extend further than to removal from Office, and disqualification to hold and enjoy any Office of honor, Trust or Profit under the United States: but the Party convicted shall nevertheless be liable and subject to Indictment, Trial, Judgment and Punishment, according to Law.

SECTION 4. The Times, Places and Manner of holding Elections for Senators and Representatives, shall be prescribed in each State by the Legislature thereof; but the Congress may at any time by Law make or alter such Regulations, except as to the Places of chusing Senators.

The Congress shall assemble at least once in every Year, and such Meeting shall be on the first Monday in December, unless they shall by Law appoint a different Day.

SECTION 5. Each Hose shall be the Judge of the elections, Returns and Qualifications of its own Members, and a Majority of each shall constitute a Quorum to do Business; but a smaller Number may adjourn from day to day, and may be authorized to compel the Attendance of absent Members, in such Manner, and under such Penalties as each House may provide.

Each House may determine the Rules of its Proceedings, punish its Members for disorderly Behavior, and, with the concurrence of two-thirds, expel a Member.

Each House shall keep a Journal of its Proceedings, and from time to time publish the same, excepting such Parts as may in their Judgment require Secrecy; and the Yeas and Nays of the Members of either House on any question shall, at the Desire of one fifth of those present, be entered on the Journal.

Neither House, during the Session of Congress, shall, without the Consent of the other, adjourn for more than three days, nor to any other Place than that in which the two Houses shall be sitting.

SECTION 6. The Senators and Representatives shall receive a Compensation for their Services, to be ascertained by Law, and paid out of the Treasury of the United States. They shall in all Cases, except Treason, Felony and Breach of the Peace, be privileged from Arrest during their Attendance at the Session of their respective Houses, and in going to and returning from the same; and for any Speech or Debate in either House, they shall not be questioned in any other Place.

No Senator or Representative shall, during the Time for which he was elected be appointed to any civil Office under the Authority of the United States, which shall have been created, or the Emoluments whereof shall have been increased during such time; and no Person holding any Office under the United States, shall be a Member of either House during his Continuance in Office.

SECTION 7. All Bills for raising Revenue shall originate in the Hose of Representatives; but the Senate may propose or concur with Amendments as on other Bills.

Every Bill which shall have passed the House of Representatives and the Senate, shall, before it became a Law, be presented to the President of the United States; if he approves he shall sign it, but if not he shall return it, with his Objections to that House in which it shall have originated, who shall enter the Objections at large on their Journal, and proceed to reconsider it. If after such Reconsideration two-thirds of that House shall agree to pass the Bill, it shall be sent, together with the Objections, to the other House, by which it shall likewise be reconsidered, and if approved by two-thirds of that House, it shall become a Law. But in all such Cases the Votes of both Houses shall be determined by Yeas and Nays, and the Names of the Persons voting for and against the Bill shall be entered on the Journal of each House, respectively. If any Bill shall not be returned by the President within ten Days (Sundays excepted) after it shall have been presented to him, the Same shall be a Law, in like Manner as if he had signed it, unless the Congress by their Adjournment prevent its Return, in which Case it shall not be a Law.

Every Order, Resolution, or Vote to which the Concurrence of the Senate and House of Representatives may be necessary (except on a question of Adjournment) shall be presented to the President of the United States; and before the Same shall take Effect, shall be approved by him, or being disapproved by him, shall be repassed by two-thirds of the Senate and House of Representatives, according to the Rules and Limitations prescribed in the Case of a Bill.

SECTION 8. The Congress shall have Power to lay and collect Taxes, Duties, Imposts and Excises, to pay the Debts and provide for the common Defence and general Welfare of the United States; but all

Duties, Imposts and Excises shall be uniform throughout the United States;

To borrow Money on the credit of the United States:

To regulate Commerce with foreign Nations, and among the several States, and with the Indian Tribes;

To establish an uniform Rule of Naturalization, and uniform Laws on the subject of Bankruptcies throughout the United States;

To coin Money, regulate the Value thereof, and of foreign Coin, and fix the Standard of Weights and Measures;

To provide for the Punishment of counterfeiting the Securities and current Coin of the United States;

To establish Post Offices and post Roads;

To promote the Progress of Science and useful Arts, by securing for limited Times to Authors and Inventors the exclusive Right to their respective Writings and Discoveries;

To constitute Tribunals inferior to the Supreme Court;

To define and punish Piracies and Felonies committed on the high Seas, and Offences against the Law of Nations;

To declare War, grant Letters of Marque and Reprisal, and make Rules concerning Captures on Land and Water;

To raise and support Armies, but no Appropriation of Money to that Use shall be for a longer Term than two Years;

To provide and maintain a Navy;

To make Rules for the Government and Regulation of the land and naval Forces;

To provide for calling forth the Militia to execute the Laws of the Union, suppress Insurrections and repel Invasions;

To provide for organizing, arming, and disciplining the Militia, and for governing such Part of them as may be employed in the Service of the United States, reserving to the States respectively, the Appointment of the Officers, and the Authority of training the Militia according to the discipline prescribed by Congress;

To exercise exclusive Legislation in all Cases whatsoever, over such District (not exceeding ten Miles square) as may, by Cession of particular States, and the Acceptance of Congress, become the Seat of the Government of the United States, and to exercise like Authority over all Places purchased by the Consent of the Legislature of the State in which the Same shall be, for the Erection of Forts, Magazines, Arsenals, dock-Yards, and other needful Buildings;—And

To make all Laws which shall be necessary and proper for carrying into Execution the foregoing Powers, and all other Powers vested by this Constitution in the Government of the United States, or in any Department or Officer thereof.

SECTION 9. The Migration or Importation of such Persons as any of the States now existing shall think proper to admit, shall not be prohibited by the Congress prior to the Year on thousand eight hundred and eight, but a Tax or duty may be imposed on such Importation, not exceeding ten dollars for each Person.

The Privilege of the Writ of Habeas Corpus shall not be suspended, unless when in Cases of Rebellion or Invasion the public Safety may require it.

No Bill of Attainder or ex post facto Law shall be passed.

No Capitation, or other direct, tax shall be laid, unless in Proportion to the Census or Enumeration herein before directed to be taken.

No Tax or Duty shall be laid on Articles exported from any State.

No Preference shall be given by any Regulation of Commerce or Revenue to the Ports of one State over those of another: nor shall Vessels bound to, or from, one State, be obliged to enter, clear, or pay Duties in another.

No Money shall be drawn from the Treasury, but in Consequence of Appropriations made by Law; regular Statement and Account of the Receipts and Expenditures of all public Money shall be published from time to time.

No Title of Nobility shall be granted by the United States: And no Person holding any Office of Profit or Trust under them, shall, without the Consent of the Congress, accept of any present, Emolument, Office, or Title, of any kind whatever, from any King, Prince, or foreign State.

SECTION 10. No State shall enter into any Treaty, Alliance, or Confederation; grant Letters of Marque and Reprisal; coin Money; emit Bills of Credit; make any Thing but gold and silver Coin a Tender in Payment of Debts; pass any bill of Attainder, ex post facto Law, or Law impairing the Obligation of Contracts, or grant any Title of Nobility.

No State shall, without the Consent of the Congress, lay any Imposts or Duties on Imports or Exports, except what may be absolutely necessary for executing its inspection Laws: and the net Produce of all Duties and Imposts, laid by any State on Imports or Exports, shall be for the use of the Treasury of the United States; and all such Laws shall be subject to the Revision and Control of the Congress.

No State shall, without the Consent of Congress, lay any Duty of Tonnage, keep Troops, or Ships of War in time of Peace, enter into any Agreement or Compact with another State, or with a foreign Power, or engage in War, unless actually invaded, or in such imminent Danger as will not admit of delay.

ARTICLE II

SECTION 1. The Executive Power shall be vested in a President of the United States of America. He shall hold his Office during the Term of four Years, and, together with the Vice President, chosen for the same Term, be elected, as follows

Each State shall appoint, in such Manner as the Legislature thereof may direct, a Number of Electors, equal to the whole Number of Senators and Representatives to which the State may be entitled in the congress: but no Senator or Representative, or Person holding an Office of Trust or Profit under the United States, shall be appointed an Elector.

The electors shall meet in their respective States, and vote by ballot for two Persons, of whom one at least shall not be an Inhabitant of the same State with themselves. And they shall make a List of all the Persons voted for, and the Number of Notes for each; which List they shall sign and certify, and transmit sealed to the Seat of the Government of the United States, directed to the President of the Senate. The President of the Senate shall, in the Presence of the Senate and House of Representatives, open all the Certificates, and the Votes shall then be counted. The Person having the greatest Number of Votes shall be the President, if such Number be a Majority of the whole Number of Electors appointed; and if there be more; than one who have such Majority, and have an equal Number of Votes, then the House of Representatives shall immediately chuse by Ballot one of them for President; and if no Person have a Majority, then from the five highest on the List the said House shall in like Manner chuse the President. But in chusing the President, the Votes shall be taken by States, the Representation from each State having one Vote; A quorum for this Purpose shall consist of a Member or Members from two-thirds of the States, and a Majority of all the States shall be necessary to a Choice. In every Case, after the choice of the President, the Person having the greatest Number of Votes of the electors shall be the Vice President. But if there should remain two or more who have equal Votes, the Senate shall chuse from them by Ballot the Vice President.

The Congress may determine the Time of chusing the Electors, and the Day on which they shall give their Votes; which Day shall be the same throughout the United States.

No Person except a natural born Citizen, or a Citizen of the United States, at the time of the Adoption of this Constitution, shall be eligible to the Office, of President; neither shall any Person be eligible to that Office who shall not have attained to the Age of thirty five Years, and been fourteen Years a Resident within the United States.

In Case of the Removal of the President from Office, or of his Death, Resignation or Inability to discharge the Powers and Duties of the said Office, the same shall devolve on the Vice President, and the Congress may by Law provide for the Case of Removal, Death, Resignation or Inability, both of the President and Vice President, declaring what Officer shall then act as President, and such Officer shall act accordingly, until the Disability be removed, or a President shall be elected.

The President shall, at stated Times, receive for his Services, a Compensation, which shall neither be increased nor diminished during the Period for which he shall have been elected, and he shall not receive within that Period any other Emolument from the United States, or any of them.

Before he enter on the Execution of his Office, he shall take the following Oath or Affirmation:—"I do solemnly swear (or affirm) that I will faithfully execute the Office of President of the United States, and will to the best of my Ability, preserve, protect and defend the Constitution of the United States."

SECTION 2. The President shall be Commander in Chief of the Army and Navy of the United States, and of the Militia of the several States, when called into the actual Service of the United States; he may require the Opinion, in writing, of the principal Officer in each of the executive Departments, upon any Subject relating to the Duties of their respective Offices, and he shall have Power to grant Reprieves and Pardons for Offences against the United States, except in Cases of Impeachment.

He shall have Power, by and with the Advice and Consent of the Senate, to make Treaties, provided two-thirds of the Senators present concur and he shall nominate, and by and with the Advice and Consent of the Senate, shall appoint Ambassadors, other public Ministers and Consuls, Judges of the supreme Court, and all other Officers of the United States, whose Appointments are not herein otherwise provided for, and which shall be established by Law: but the Congress may by Law vest the Appointment of such inferior Officers, as they think proper, in the President alone, in the Courts of Law or in the Heads of Departments.

The President shall have Power to fill up all Vacancies that may happen during the Recess of the Senate, by granting Commissions which shall expire at the End of their next Session.

SECTION 3. He shall from time to time give to the Congress Information of the State of the Union, and recommend to their Consideration such Measures as he shall judge necessary and expedient; he may, on extraordinary Occasions, convene both Houses, or either of them, and, in Case of Disagreement between them, with Respect to the Time of Adjournment, he may adjourn them to such Time as he shall think proper; he shall receive Ambassadors and other public Ministers; he shall take Care that the Laws be faithfully executed, and shall Commission all the Officers of the United States.

SECTION 4. The President, Vice President and all civil Officers of the United States, shall be removed from Office on Impeachment for, and Conviction of, Treason, Bribery, or other high Crimes and Misdemeanors.

ARTICLE III

SECTION 1.The judicial Power of the United States, shall be vested in one supreme Court, and in such inferior Courts as the Congress may from time to time ordain and establish. The Judges, both of the supreme and inferior Courts, shall hold their Offices during good Behaviour, and shall, at stated Times, receive for their Services, a Compensation, which shall not be diminished during their Continuance in Office.

SECTION 2. The judicial Power shall extend to all Cases, in Law and Equity, arising under this Constitution, the Laws of the United States, and Treaties made, or which shall be made, under their Authority;—

to all Cases of admiralty and maritime Jurisdiction;—to Controversies to which the United States shall be a Party;—to Controversies between two or more States;—between a State and Citizens of another State;—between Citizens of the same State claiming Lands under Grants of different States, and between a State, or the Citizens thereof, and foreign States, Citizens or Subjects.

In all Cases affecting Ambassadors, other public Ministers and Consuls, and those in which a State shall be Party, the Supreme Court shall have original Jurisdiction. In all other Cases before mentioned, the supreme Court shall have appellate Jurisdiction, both as to Law and Fact, with such Exceptions, and under such Regulations as the Congress shall make.

The Trial of all Crimes, except in Cases of Impeachment, shall be by Jury; and such Trial shall be held in the State where the said Crimes shall have been committed; but when not committed within any State, the Trial shall be at such Place or Places as the Congress may be Law have directed.

SECTION 3. Treason against the United States shall consist only in levying War against them, or in adhering to their Enemies, giving them Aid and Comfort. No Person shall be convicted of Treason unless on the Testimony of two Witnesses to the same overt Act, or on Confession in open Court.

The Congress shall have Power to declare the Punishment of Treason, but no Attainder of Treason shall work Corruption of Blood, or Forfeiture except during the Life of the Person attainted.

ARTICLE IV

SECTION1. Full Faith and Credit shall be given in each State to the public Acts, Records, and judicial Proceedings of every other State And the Congress may be general Laws prescribe the Manner in which such Acts, Records and Proceedings shall be proved, and the Effect thereof.

SECTION 2. The Citizens of each State shall be entitled to all Privileges and Immunities of Citizens in the several States.

A person charged in any State with Treason, Felony, or other Crime, who shall flee from Justice, and be found in another State, shall on Demand of the executive Authority of the State from which he fled, be delivered up, to be removed to the State having Jurisdiction of the Crime.

No Person held to Service or Labour in one State, under the Laws thereof, escaping into another, shall, in Consequence of any Law or Regulation therein, be discharged from such Service or Labour, but shall be delivered up on Claim of the Party to whom such Service or Labour may be due.

SECTION 3. New States may be admitted by the Congress into this Union; but no new State shall be formed or erected within the Jurisdiction of any other State; nor any State be formed by the Junction of two or more States, or Parts of States, without the Consent of the Legislatures of the States concerned as well as of the Congress.

The Congress shall have Power to dispose of and make all needful Rules and Regulations respecting the Territory or other Property belonging to the United States; and nothing in this Constitution shall be so construed as to Prejudice any Claims of the United States, or of any particular State.

SECTION 4. The United States shall guarantee to every State in this Union a Republican Form of Government, and shall protect each of them against Invasion; and on Application of the Legislature, or of the Executive (when the Legislature cannot be convened) against domestic Violence.

ARTICLE V

The Congress, whenever two-thirds of both houses shall deem it necessary, shall propose Amendments to this Constitution, or, on the Application of the Legislatures of two-thirds of the several States, shall call a Convention for proposing Amendments, which, in either Case, shall be valid to all Intents and Purposes, as Part of this Constitution, when ratified by the Legislatures of three fourths of the several States, or by Conventions in three fourths thereof, as the one or the other Mode of Ratification may be proposed by the Congress; Provided that no Amendment which may be made prior to the year One thousand eight hundred and eight shall in any Manner affect the first and fourth Clauses in the Ninth Section of the first Article; and that no State, without its Consent, shall be deprived of its equal Suffrage in the Senate.

ARTICLE VI

All Debts contracted and Engagements entered into, before the Adoption of this Constitution, shall be valid against the United States under this Constitution, as under the Confederation.

This Constitution, and the Laws of the United States which shall be made in Pursuance thereof; and all Treaties made, or which shall be made, under the Authority of the United States, shall be the supreme Law of the Land; and the Judges in every State shall be bound thereby, any Thing in the Constitution or Laws of any State to the Contrary notwithstanding.

The Senators and Representatives before mentioned, and the Members of the several State Legislatures, and all executive and judicial Officers, both of the United States and of the several States, shall be bound by Oath or Affirmation, to support this Constitution; but no religious Test shall ever be required as a Qualification to any Office or public Trust under the United States.

ARTICLE VII

The Ratification of the Conventions of nine States, shall be sufficient for the Establishment of this Constitution between the States so ratifying the Same.

DONE in Convention by the Unanimous Consent of the States present the Seventeenth Day of September in the year of our Lord one thousand seven hundred and Eighty seven and of the Independence of the United States of America the Twelfth. IN WITNESS whereof We have hereunto subscribed our Names.

G° WASHINGTON
Presid[t] and deputy from Virginia

AMENDMENTS

ARTICLE I

[THE FIRST TEN ARTICLES PROPOSED 25 SEPTEMBER 1789; DECLARED IN FORCE 15 DECEMBER 1791]

Congress shall make no law respecting an establishment of religion, or prohibiting the free exercise thereof; or abridging the freedom of speech, or of the press; or the right of the people peaceably to assemble, and to petition the Government for a redress of grievances.

ARTICLE II

A well regulated Militia, being necessary to the security of a free State, the right of the people to keep and bear Arms, shall not be infringed.

ARTICLE III

No Soldier shall, in time of peace, be quartered in any house, without the consent of the Owner, nor in time of war, but in a manner to be prescribed by law.

ARTICLE IV

The right of the people to be secure in their persons, houses, papers, and effects, against unreasonable searches and seizures, shall not be violated, and no Warrants shall issue, but upon probable cause, supported by Oath or affirmation, and particularly describing the place to be searched, and the persons or things to be seized.

ARTICLE V

No person shall be held to answer for a capital, or otherwise infamous crime, unless on a presentment or indictment of a Grand Jury, except in cases arising in the land or naval forces, or in the Militia, when in actual service in time of War or public danger; nor shall any person be subject for the same offence to be twice put in jeopardy of like or limb; nor shall be compelled in any Criminal Case to be a witness against himself, nor be deprived of like, liberty, or property, without due process of law; nor shall private property be taken for public use, without just compensation.

ARTICLE VI

In all criminal prosecutions, the accused shall enjoy the right to a speedy and public trial, by an impartial jury of the State and district wherein the crime shall have been committed, which district shall have been previously ascertained by law, and to be informed of the nature and cause of the accusation; to be confronted with the witnesses against him; to have compulsory process for obtaining Witnesses in his favor, and to have the Assistance of Counsel for his defence.

ARTICLE VII

In suits at common law, where the value in controversy shall exceed twenty dollars, the right of trial by jury shall be preserved, and no fact by a jury shall be otherwise re-examined in any Court of the United States, than according to the rules of the common law.

ARTICLE VIII

Excessive bail shall not be required, nor excessive fines imposed, nor cruel and unusual punishments inflicted.

ARTICLE IX

The enumeration in the Constitution, of certain rights, shall not be construed to deny or disparage others retained by the people.

ARTICLE X

The powers not delegated to the United States by the Constitution, nor prohibited by it to the States, are reserved to the States respectively, or to the people.

ARTICLE XI

[PROPOSED 5 MARCH 1794; DECLARED RATIFIED 8 JANUARY 1798]

The Judicial power of the United States shall not be construed to extend to any suit in law or equity, commenced or prosecuted against one of the United States by Citizens of another State, or by Citizens or Subjects of any Foreign State.

ARTICLE XII

[PROPOSED 1 DECEMBER 1803; DECLARED RATIFIED 25 SEPTEMBER 1804]

The Electors shall meet in their respective states, and note by ballot for President and Vice-President, one of whom, at least, shall not be an inhabitant of the same state with themselves; they shall name in their ballots the person voted for as President, and in distinct ballots the person voted for as Vice-President, and they shall make distinct lists of all persons voted for as President, and of all persons voted for as Vice-President, and of the number of votes for each, which lists they shall sign and certify, and transmit sealed to the seat of the Government of the United States, directed to the President of the Senate;—The President of the Senate shall, in the presence of the Senate and House of Representatives, open all the certificates and the votes shall then be counted;—The person having the greatest number of votes for President, shall be the President, if such number be a majority of the whole number of Electors appointed; and if no person have such majority, then from the persons having the highest numbers not exceeding three on the list of those voted for as President, the House of Representatives shall choose immediately, by ballot, the President. But in choosing the President, the votes shall be taken by states, the representation from each state having one vote; a quorum for this purpose shall consist of a member or members from two-thirds of the states, and a majority of all the states shall be necessary to a choice. And if the House of Representatives shall not choose a President whenever the right of choice shall devolve upon them, before the fourth day of March next following, then the Vice-President shall act as President, as in the case of death or other constitutional disability of the President. The person having the greatest number of votes as Vice-President, shall be the Vice-President, if such number be a majority of the whole number of Electors appointed, and if no person have a majority, then from the two highest numbers on the list, the Senate shall choose the Vice-President; a quorum for the purpose shall consist of two-thirds of the whole number of Senators, and a majority of the stitutionally ineligible to the office of President shall be eligible to that of Vice-President of the United States.

ARTICLE XIII

[PROPOSED 1 FEBRUARY 1865; DECLARED RATIFIED 18 DECEMBER 1866]

SECTION 1. Neither slavery nor involuntary servitude, except as a punishment for crime whereof the party shall have been duly convicted, shall exist within the United States, or any place subject to their jurisdiction.

SECTION 2. Congress shall have power to enforce this article by appropriate legislation.

ARTICLE XIV

[PROPOSED 16 JUNE 1866; DECLARED RATIFIED 28 JULY 1868]

SECTION 1. All persons born or naturalized in the United States, and subject to the jurisdiction thereof, are citizens of the United States and of the State wherein they reside. No State shall make or enforce any law which shall abridge the privileges or immunities of citizens of the United States; nor shall any State deprive any person of like, liberty, or property, without due process of law; nor deny to any person within its jurisdiction the equal protection of the laws.

SECTION 2. Representatives shall be apportioned among the several States according to their respective numbers, counting the whole number of persons in each State, excluding Indians not taxed. But when the right to vote at any election for the choice of electors for President and Vice President of the United States, Representatives in Congress, the Executive and Judicial officers of a State, or the members of the Legislature thereof, is denied to any of the male inhabitants of such State, being twenty-one years of age, and citizens of the United States, or in any way abridged, except for participation in rebellion, or other crime, the basis of representation therein shall be reduced in the proportion which the number of such male citizens shall bear to the whole number of male citizens twenty-one years of age in such State.

SECTION 3. No person shall be a Senator or Representative in Congress, or elector of President and Vice President, or hold any office, civil, or military, under the United States, or under any State, who, having previously taken an oath, as a member of Congress, or as an officer of the United States, or as a member of any State legislature, or as an executive or judicial officer of any State, to support the Constitution of the United States, shall have engaged in insurrection or rebellion against the same, or given aid or comfort to the enemies thereof. But Congress may by a vote of two-thirds of each House, remove such disability.

SECTION 4. The validity of the public debt of the United States, authorized by law, including debts incurred for payment of pensions and bounties for services in suppressing insurrection or rebellion, shall not be questioned. But neither the United States nor any State shall assume or pay any debt or obligation incurred in aid of insurrection or rebellion against the United States, or any claim for the loss or emancipation of any slave; but all such debts, obligations and claims shall be held illegal and void.

SECTION 5. The Congress shall have power to enforce, by appropriate legislation, the provisions of this article.

ARTICLE XV

[PROPOSED 27 FEBRUARY 1869; DECLARED RATIFIED 30 MARCH 1870]

SECTION 1. The right of citizens of the United States to vote shall not be denied or abridged by the United States or by any State on account of race, color, or previous condition of servitude.

SECTION2. The Congress shall have power to enforce this article by appropriate legislation.

ARTICLE XVI

[PROPOSED 12 JULY 1909; DECLARED RATIFIED 25 FEBRUARY 1913]

The Congress shall have power to lay and collect taxes on incomes, from whatever source derived, without apportionment among the several States, and without regard to any census or enumeration.

ARTICLE XVII

[PROPOSED 16 MAY 1912; DECLARED RATIFIED 31 MAY 1913]

The Senate of the United States shall be composed of two senators from each State, elected by the people thereof, for six years; and each Senator shall have one vote. The electors in each State shall have the qualifications requisite for electors of the most numerous branch of the State legislature.

When vacancies happen in the representation of any State in the Senate, the executive authority of such State shall issue writs of election to fill such vacancies: PROVIDED, That the legislature of any State may empower the executive thereof to make temporary appointments until the people fill the vacancies by election as the legislature may direct.

This amendment shall not be so construed as to affect the election or term of any senator chosen before it becomes valid as part of the Constitution.

ARTICLE XVIII

[PROPOSED 18 DECEMBER 1917; DECLARED RATIFIED 29 JANUARY 1919]

After one year from the ratification of this article, the manufacture, sale, or transportation of intoxicating liquors within, the importation thereof into, or the exportation thereof from the United States and all territory subject to the jurisdiction thereof for beverage purposes is hereby prohibited.

The Congress and the several States shall have concurrent power to enforce this article by appropriate legislation.

This article shall be inoperative unless it shall have been ratified as an amendment to the Constitution by the legislatures of the several States, as provided in the Constitution, within seven years from the date of the submission hereof to the States by the Congress.

ARTICLE XIX

[PROPOSED 4 JUNE 1919; DECLARED RATIFIED 26 AUGUST 1920]

The right of citizens of the United States to vote shall not be denied or abridged by the United States or by any States on account of sex.

The Congress shall have power, by appropriate legislation, to enforce the provisions of this article.

ARTICLE XX

[PROPOSED 2 MARCH 1932; DECLARED RATIFIED 6 FEBRUARY 1933]

SECTION 1. The terms of the President and Vice-President shall end at noon on the twentieth day of January, and the terms of Senators and Representatives at noon on the third day of January, of the years in which such terms would have ended if this article had not been ratified; and the terms of their successors shall then begin.

SECTION 2. The Congress shall assemble at least once in every year, and such meeting shall begin at noon on the third day of January, unless they shall by law appoint a different day.

SECTION 3. If, at the time fixed for the beginning of the term of the President, the President-elect shall have died, the Vice-President-elect shall become President. If a President shall not have been chosen before the time fixed for the beginning of his term, or if the president-elect shall have failed to qualify, then the vice-President-elect shall act as President until a President shall have qualified; and the Congress may by law provide for the case wherein neither a President-elect nor a Vice-President-elect shall have qualified, declaring who shall then act as President, or the manner in which one who is to act shall be selected, and such person shall act accordingly until a President or Vice-President shall have qualified.

SECTION 4. The Congress may by law provide for the case of the death of any of the persons from whom the House of Representatives may choose a President whenever the right of choice shall have devolved upon them, and for the case of the death of any of the persons from whom the Senate may choose a Vice-President whenever the right of choice shall have devolved upon them.

SECTION 5. Sections 1 and 2 shall take effect on the 15th day of October following the ratification of this article.

SECTION 6. This article shall be inoperative unless it shall have been ratified as an amendment to the Constitution by the legislatures of three-fourths of the several States within seven years from the date of its submission.

ARTICLE XXI

[PROPOSED 20 FEBRUARY 1933; ADOPTED 5 DECEMBER 1933]

SECTION 1. The eighteenth article of amendment to the Constitution of the United States is hereby repealed.

SECTION 2. The transportation or importation into any State, Territory or possession of the United States for delivery or use therein of intoxicating liquors, in violation of the laws thereof, is hereby prohibited.

SECTION 3. This article shall be inoperative unless it shall have been ratified as an amendment to the Constitution by the legislatures of three-fourths of the several States within seven years from the date of its submission.

ARTICLE XXII

[PROPOSED 24 MARCH 1947; ADOPTED 26 FEBRUARY 1951]

SECTION 1. No person shall be elected to the office of the President more than twice, and no person who has held the office of President, or acted as president, for more than two years of a term to which some other person was elected President shall be elected to the office of the President more than once. But this Article shall not apply to any person holding the office of President when this Article was proposed by the Congress, and shall not prevent any person who may be holding the office of President, or acting as President, during the term within which this Article becomes operative from holding the office of president or acting as President during the remainder of such term.

ARTICLE XXIII

[PROPOSED 6 JANUARY 1960; ADOPTED 3 APRIL 1961]

SECTION 1. The District constituting the seat of Government of the United States shall appoint in such manner as the Congress may direct:

A number of electors of President and Vice President equal to the whole number of Senators and Representatives in Congress to which the District would be entitled if it were a State, but in no event more than the least populous State; they shall be considered, for the purposes of the election of President and Vice President, to be electors appointed by a State; and they shall meet in the District and perform such duties as provided by the twelfth article of amendment.

SECTION 2. The Congress shall have power to enforce this article by appropriate legislation.

APPENDIX II

CONSTITUTION OF THE REPUBLIC OF TURKEY
(Selections)

(As amended on 23 July 1995 under Law No. 4121/1)

PREAMBLE

In line with the concept of nationalism outlined and the reforms and principles introduced by the founder of the Republic of Turkey, Atatürk, the immortal leader and the unrivaled hero, this Constitution, which affirms the eternal existence of the Turkish nation and motherland and the indivisible unity of the Turkish State, embodies;

The determination to safeguard the everlasting existence, prosperity and material and spiritual well-being of the Republic of Turkey and to attain the standards of contemporary civilization as an honourable member with equal rights of the family of world nations;

The understanding of the absolute supremacy of the will of nation and of the fact that sovereignty is vested fully and unconditionally in the Turkish nation and that no individual or body empowered to exercise this sovereignty in the name of the nation shall deviate from liberal democracy and the legal system instituted according to its requirements;

The principle of the separation of powers, which does not imply an order of precedence among the organs of State but refers solely to the exercising of certain State powers and discharging duties, which are limited to cooperation and division of functions, and which accepts the supremacy of the Constitution and the law;

The recognition that no protection shall be accorded to thoughts or opinions contrary to Turkish national interests, the principle of the indivisibility of the existence of Turkey with its State and territory, Turkish historical and moral values or the nationalism, principles, reforms and modernism of Atatürk and that , as required by the principle of secularism, there shall be no interference whatsoever of the sacred religious feelings in State affairs and politics; The acknowledgment that it is the birthright of every Turkish citizen to lead an honourable life and to develop his/her material and spiritual assets under the aegis of national culture, civilization and the rule of law, through the exercise of the fundamental rights and freedoms set forth in this Constitution in conformity with the requirements of equality and social justice;

The recognition that all Turkish citizens are united in national honour and pride, in national joy and grief, in their rights and duties regarding national existence, in blessings and in burdens, and in every manifestation of national life, and that they have the right to demand a peaceful life based on absolute respect for one another's rights and freedoms, mutual love and fellowship and the desire for a belief in "Peace at home, peace in the world";

This Constitution, which is to be embraced with the ideas, beliefs, and resolutions it embodies below should be interpreted and implemented accordingly commanding respect for, and absolute loyalty to, its letter and spirit,

Is entrusted by the Turkish nation to the patriotism and nationalism of its democracy-loving sons and daughters.

PART ONE
GENERAL PRINCIPLES

I. Form of the State

ARTICLE 1. The Turkish State is a Republic.

II. Characteristics of the Republic

ARTICLE 2. The Republic of Turkey is a democratic, secular and social State governed by the rule of law; bearing in mind the concepts of public peace, national solidarity and justice; respecting human rights; loyal to the nationalism of Atatürk, and based on the fundamental tenets set forth in the Preamble.

III. Integrity of the State, Official Language, Flag, National Anthem, and Capital

ARTICLE 3. The Turkish State, with its territory and nation, is an indivisible entity. Its language is Turkish.

Its flag, the form of which is prescribed by the relevant law, is composed of a white crescent and star on a red background.

Its national anthem is the "Independence March."

Its capital is Ankara.

ARTICLE 4. The provision of Article 1 of the Constitution establishing the form of the State as a Republic, the provisions in Article 2 on the characteristics of the Republic, and the provision of Article 3 shall not be amended, nor shall their amendment be proposed.

V. Fundamental Aims and Duties of the State

ARTICLE 5. The fundamental aims and duties of the State are; to safeguard the independence and integrity of the Turkish Nation, the indivisibility of the country, the Republic and democracy; to ensure the welfare, peace, and happiness of the individual and society; to strive for the removal of political, social and economic obstacles which restrict the fundamental rights and freedoms of the individual in a manner incompatible with the principles of justice and of the social State governed by the rule of law; and to provide the conditions required for the development of the individual" material and spiritual existence.

VI. Sovereignty

ARTICLE 6. Sovereignty is vested fully and unconditionally in the nation.

The Turkish Nation shall exercise its sovereignty through the authorised organs as prescribed by the principles laid down in the Constitution.

The right to exercise sovereignty shall not be delegated to any individual, group or class. No person or agency shall exercise any State authority which does not emanate from the Constitution.

VII. Legislative Power

ARTICLE 7. Legislative power is vested in the Turkish Grand National Assembly on behalf of the Turkish Nation. This power cannot be delegated.

VIII. Executive Power and Function

ARTICLE 8. Executive power and function shall be exercised and carried out by the President of the Republic and the Council of Ministers in conformity with the Constitution and the law.

IX. Judicial Power

ARTICLE 9. Judicial power shall be exercised by independent courts on behalf of the Turkish Nation.

X. Equality before the Law

ARTICLE 10. All individuals are equal without any discrimination before the law, irrespective of language, race, colour, sex, political opinion, philosophical belief, religion and sect, or any such considerations.

No privilege shall be granted to any individual, family, group or class.

State organs and administrative authorities shall act in compliance with the principle of equality before the law in all their proceedings.

IX. Supremacy and Binding Force of the Constitution

ARTICLE 11. The provisions of the Constitution are fundamental legal rules binding upon legislative, executive and judicial organs, and administrative authorities and other institutions and individuals.

Laws shall not be in conflict with the Constitution.

PART TWO
FUNDAMENTAL RIGHTS AND DUTIES

CHAPTER ONE

GENERAL PROVISIONS

Nature of Fundamental Rights and Freedoms

ARTICLE 12. Everyone possesses inherent fundamental rights and freedoms which are inviolable and inalienable.

The fundamental rights and freedoms also comprise the duties and individuals.

II. Restriction of Fundamental Rights and Freedoms

ARTICLE 13. Fundamental rights and freedoms may be restricted by law, in conformity with the letter and spirit of the Constitution, with the aim of safeguarding the indivisible integrity of the State with its territory and nation, national sovereignty, the Republic, national security, public order, general peace, the public interest, public morals and public health, and also for specific reasons set forth in the relevant Articles of the Constitution.

General and specific grounds for restrictions of fundamental rights and freedoms shall not conflict with the requirements of the democratic order of society and shall not be imposed for any purpose other than those for which they are prescribed.

The general grounds for restriction set forth in this article shall apply for all fundamental rights and freedoms.

Prohibition of Abuse of Fundamental Rights and Freedoms

ARTICLE 14. None of the rights and freedoms embodied in the Constitution shall be exercised with the aim of violating the indivisible integrity of the State with its territory and nation, of endangering the existence of the Turkish State and Republic, of destroying fundamental rights and freedoms, of placing the government of the State under the control of an individual or a group, or establishing the hegemony of one social class over the others, or creating discrimination on the basis of language, race, religion or sect, or of establishing by any other means a system of government based on these concepts and ideas.

The sanctions to be applied against those who violate these prohibitions, and those who incite and provoke others to the same end shall be determined by law.

No provision of this Constitution shall be interpreted in a manner that would grant the right of destroying the rights and freedoms embodied in the Constitution.

IV. Suspension of the Exercise of Fundamental Rights and Freedoms

ARTICLE 15. In times of war, mobilization, martial law, or state of emergency, the exercise of fundamental rights and freedoms can be partially or entirely suspended, or measures may be taken, to the extent required by the exigencies of the situation, which derogate the guarantees embodied in the Constitution, provided that obligations under international law are not violates.

Even under the circumstances indicated in the first paragraph, the individual's right to life, and the integrity of his/her material and spiritual entity shall be inviolable except where death occurs through lawful act of warfare and execution of death sentences; no one may be compelled to reveal his/her religion, conscience, thought or opinion, nor be accused on account of them; offences and penalties may not be made retrocative, nor may anyone be held guilty until so proven by a court judgment.

V. Status of Aliens

ARTICLE 16. The fundamental rights and freedoms of aliens may be restricted by law in a manner consistent with international law.

CHAPTER TWO

THE RIGHTS AND DUTIES OF THE INDIVIDUAL

I. Personal Inviolability, Material and Spiritual Entity of the individual

ARTICLE 17. Everyone has the right to life and the right to protect and develop his material and spiritual entity.

The physical integrity of the individual shall not be violated except under medical necessity and in cases prescribed by law; and shall not be subjected to scientific or medical experiments without his/her consent.

No one shall be subjected to torture or ill-treatment; no one shall be subjected to penalties or treatment incompatible with human dignity.

Cases such as the execution of death penalties under court sentences, the act of killing in self-defense, ocurrences of death as a result of the use of a weapon permitted by law as a necessary measure during apprehension, the execution of warrants of arrest, the prevention of the flee of lawfully arrested or convicted persons, the quelling of a riot or insurrection, or carrying out the orders of authorized bodies during martial law or state of emergency, are outside of the scope of the provision of paragraph 1.

II. Prohibition of Forced Labour

ARTICLE 18. No one shall be forced to work. Corvee is prohibited.

Work required of an individual while serving a court sentence or under detention, services required from citizens during a state of emergency, and physical or intellectual work necessitated by the requirements of the country as a civic obligation, provided that the form and conditions of such labour are prescribed by law.

III. Personal Liberty and Security

ARTICLE 19. Everyone has the right to liberty and security of person.

No one shall be deprived of his/her liberty except in the following cases where procedure and conditions are prescribed by law: Execution of sentences restricting liberty and the implementation of security measurers decided by court order; apprehension or detention of an individual in line with a court ruling or an obligation upon him designated by law execution of an order for the purpose of the educational supervision of a minor or for bringing him/her before the competent authority; execution of measures taken in conformity with the relevant legal provision for the treatment, education or correction in institutions of a person of unsound mind, an alcoholic or drug addict or vagrant or a person spreading contagious diseases, when such persons constitute a danger to the public, apprehension or detention of a person who enters or attempts to enter illegally into the country or for whom a deportation or extradition order has been issued.

Individuals against whom there are strong indications of having committed an offence can be arrested by decision of a judge solely for the purposes of preventing escape, or preventing the destruction or alteration of evidence as well as in similar other circumstances which necessitate detention and are prescribed by law. Apprehension of a person without a decision by a judge shall be resorted to only in cases when a person is caught in the act of committing an offence or in cases where delay is likely to thwart justice; the conditions for such acts shall be defined by law. Individuals arrested or detained shall be promptly notified, and in all cases in writing, or orally, when the former is not possible, of the grounds for their arrest or detention and the charges against them; in cases of offences committed collectively this notification shall be made, at the latest, before the individual is brought before a judge.

The person arrested or detained shall be brought before a judge within forty-eight hours and in the case of offences committed collectively within fifteen days, excluding the time taken to send him to the court nearest to the place of arrest. No one can be deprived of his/her liberty without the decision of a judge after the expiry of the above specified periods. These periods may be extended during a state of emergency, under martial law or in time of war.

Notification of the situation of the person arrested or detained shall be made to the next of kin, except in cases of definite necessity pertaining to the risks of revealing the scope and subject of the investigation compelling otherwise.

Persons under detention shall have the right to request to be tried within a reasonable time or to be released during investigation or prosecution. Release may be made conditional to the presentation of an appropriate guarantee with a view to securing the presence of the person at the trial proceedings and the execution of the court sentence.

Persons deprived of their liberty under any circumstances are entitled to apply to the appropriate judicial authority for speedy conclusion of proceedings regarding their situation and for their release if the restriction placed upon them is not lawful.

Damages suffered by persons subjected to treatment contrary to the above provisions shall be compensated for according to law, by the State.

IV. Privacy and Protection of Private Life

A. Privacy of the Individual's Life

ARTICLE 20. Everyone has the right to demand respect for his/her private and family life. Privacy of individual and family life cannot be violated. Exceptions necessitated by judiciary investigation and prosecution are reserved.

Unless there exists a decision duly passed by a judge in cases explicitly defined by law, and unless there exists an order of an agency authorised by law in cases where delay is deemed prejudicial, neither the person nor the private papers, not belongings of an individual shall be searched nor shall they be seized.

B. Inviolability of Domicile

ARTICLE 21. The domicile of an individual shall not be violated. Unless there exists a decision duly passed by a judge in cases explicitly defined by law, and unless there exists an order of an agency authorised by law in cases where delay is deemed prejudicial, no domicile may be entered or searched, or the property therein seized.

C. Freedom of Communication

ARTICLE 22. Everyone has the right to freedom of communication.

Secrecy of communication is fundamental.

Communication shall not be impeded nor its secrecy be violated, unless there exists a decision duly passed by a judge in cases explicitly defined by law, and unless there exists an order of an agency authorized by law in cases where delay is deemed prejudicial.

Public establishments or institutions where exceptions to the above may be applied will be defined by law.

V. Freedom of Residence and Movement

ARTICLE 23. Everyone has the right to freedom of residence and movement.

Freedom of residence may be restricted by law for the purpose of preventing offences, promoting social and economic development, ensuring sound and orderly urban growth, and protecting public property; freedom of movement may be restricted by law for the purpose of investigation and prosecution of an offence, and prevention of offences. A citizen's freedom to leave the country may be restricted on account of the national economic situation, civic obligations, or criminal investigation or prosecution.

Citizens may not be deported, or deprived of their right of entry into their homeland.

VI. Freedom of Religion and Conscience

ARTICLE 24. Everyone has the right to freedom of conscience, religious belief and conviction.

Acts of worship, religious services, and ceremonies shall be conducted freely, provided that they do not violate the provisions of Article 14.

No one shall be compelled to worship, or to participate in religious ceremonies and rites, to reveal religious beliefs and convictions, or be blamed or accused because of his religious beliefs and convictions.

Education and instruction in religion and ethics shall be conducted under State supervision and control. Instruction in religious culture and moral education shall be compulsory in the curricula of primary and secondary schools. Other religious education and instruction shall be subject to the individual's own desire, and in the case of minors, to the request of their legal representatives.

No one shall be allowed to exploit or abuse religion or religious feelings, or things held sacred by religion, in any manner whatsoever, for the purpose of personal or political influence, or for even partially basing the fundamental, social, economic, political, and legal order of the State on religious tenets.

VII. Freedom of Thought and Opinion

ARTICLE 25. Everyone has the right to freedom of thought and opinion.

No one shall be compelled to reveal his thoughts and opinions for any reason or purpose, nor shall anyone be blamed or accused on account of his thought and opinions.

VIII. Freedom of Expression and Dissemination of Thought

ARTICLE 26. Everyone has the right to express and disseminate his thoughts and opinion by speech, in writing or in pictures or through other media, individually or collectively. This right includes the freedom to receive and impart information and ideas without interference from official authorities. This provision shall not preclude subjecting transmission by radio, television, cinema, and similar means to a system of licensing.

The exercise of these freedoms may be restricted for the purposes of preventing crime, punishing offenders, withholding information duly classified as a State secret, protecting the reputation and rights and the private and family life of others, or protecting professional secrets as prescribed by law, or enduring the proper functioning of the judiciary.

No language prohibited by law shall be used in the expression and dissemination of thought. Any written or printed documents, phonograph records, magnetic or video tapes, and other means of expression used in contravention of this provision shall be seized by a duly issued decision of a judge or, in cases where delay is deemed prejudicial, by the competent authority designated by law. The authority issuing the seizure order shall notify the competent judge of its decision within twenty-four hours. The judge shall decide on the matter within three days.

Provisions regulating the use of means of disseminating information and ideas shall not be interpreted as a restriction of freedom of expression and dissemination unless they prevent the dissemination of information and thought.

IX. Freedom of Science and Arts

ARTICLE 27. Everyone has the right to study and teach freely, explain, and disseminate science and arts and to carry out research in these fields.

The right to disseminate shall not be exercised for the purpose of changing the provisions of Articles 1, 2 and 3 of this Constitution.

The provisions of this article shall not preclude regulation by law of the entry and distribution of foreign publications in the country.

X. Provisions Relating to the Press and Publication

A. Freedom of the Press

ARTICLE 28. The press is free, and shall not be censored. The establishment of a printing house shall not be subject to prior permission or the deposit of a financial guarantee.

Publication shall not be made in any language prohibited by law.

The State shall take the necessary measures to ensure the freedom of the press and freedom of information.

In the limitation of freedom of the press, Articles 26 and 27 of the Constitution are applicable.

Anyone who writes or prints any news or articles which threaten the internal or external security of the State or the indivisible integrity of the State with its territory and nation, which tend to incite offence, riot or insurrection, or which refer to classified State secrets and anyone who prints or transmits such news or articles to others for the above purposes, shall be held responsible under the law relevant to these offences. Distribution may be suspended as a preventive measure by the decision of a judge, or in the event delay is deemed prejudicial, by the competent authority designated by law. The authority suspending distribution shall notify a competent judge of its decision within twenty-four hours at the latest. The order suspending distribution shall become null and void unless upheld by a competent judge within forty-eight hours at the latest.

No ban shall be placed on the reporting of events, except by the decision of judge issued to ensure proper functioning of the judiciary, within the limits specified by law.

Periodical and non-periodical publications may be seized by a decision of a judge in cases of ongoing investigation or prosecution of offences prescribed by law, and, in situations where delay could endanger the indivisible integrity of the State with its territory and nation, national security, public order or public morals and for the prevention of offence by order or public morals and for the prevention of offence by order of the competent authority designated by law. The authority issuing the seizure order shall notify a competent judge of its decision within twenty-four hours at the latest. The seizure order shall become null and void unless upheld by the competent court within forty-eight hours at the latest.

The general common provisions shall apply when seizure and confiscation of periodicals and non-periodicals for reasons of criminal investigation and prosecution take place.

Periodicals published in Turkey may be temporarily suspended by court sentence if found guilty of publishing material which contravenes the indivisible integrity of the State with its territory and nation, the fundamental principles of the Republic, national security and public morals. Any publication which clearly bears the characteristics of being a continuation of a suspended periodical is prohibited, and shall be seized following a decision by a competent judge.

CHAPTER FOUR

POLITICAL RIGHTS AND DUTIES

I. Turkish Citizenship

ARTICLE 66. Everyone bound to the Turkish State through the bond of citizenship is a Turk.

The child of a Turkish father or a Turkish mother is a Turk. The citizenship of a child of a foreign father and a Turkish mother shall be defined by law.

Citizenship can be acquired under the conditions stipulated by law, and shall be forteited only in cases determined by law.

No Turk shall be deprived of citizenship, unless he commits an act incompatible with loyalty to the motherland.

Recourse to the courts, against the decisions and proceedings related to the deprivation of citizenship, shall not be denied.

II. Right to Vote, to Be Elected and to Engage in Political Activity

ARTICLE 67. In conformity with the conditions set forth in the law, citizens have the right to vote, to be elected, and to engage in political activities independently or in a political party, and to take part in a referendum.

(Amended: 23.7.1995 – 4121/5 Article) Elections and referenda shall be held under the direction and supervision of the judiciary, in accordance with the principles of free, equal, secret, and direct, universal suffrage, and public counting of the votes. However, the conditions under which the Turkish citizens who are abroad shall be able to exercise their right to vote, are regulated by law.

(Amended: 23.7.1995 – 4121/5 Article) All Turkish citizens over 18 years of age shall have the right to vote in elections and to take part in referenda.

The exercise of these rights shall be regulated by law.

(Amended: 23.7.1995 – 4121/5 Article) Private and corporals serving in the armed services, students in military schools and convicts in penal execution institutions cannot vote. The Supreme Election Council shall determine the measures to be taken to ensure the safety of the counting of votes when detainees in penal execution institutions or persons exercise their right to vote; such voting is

done under the on-site direction and supervision of authorized judge.

(Annexation: 23.7.1995 – 4121/5 Article) The electoral laws shall be drawn up in such a way as to reconcile the principles of fair representation and consistency in administration.

III. Provisions Relating to Political Parties

A. Forming Parties, Membership and Withdrawal From Membership in a Party

ARTICLE 68. *Amended: 23.7.1995 – 4121/6 Article) Citizens have the right to form political parties and in accordance with the established procedure to join and withdraw from them. One must be over 18 years of age to become a member of a party.*

Political parties are indispensable elements of the democratic political life.

Political parties shall be formed without prior permission and shall pursue their activities in accordance with the provisions set forth in the Constitution and law.

The statutes and programmes, as well as the activities of political parties shall not be in conflict with the independence of the State, its indivisible integrity with its territory and nation, human rights, the principles of equality and rule of law, sovereignty of the nation, the principles of the democratic and secular republic; they shall not aim to protect or establish class or group dictatorship or dictatorship of any kind, nor shall they incite citizens to crime.

Judges and prosecutors, members of higher judicial organs including those of the Court of Accounts, civil servants in public institutions and organizations, other public servants who are not yet in higher education institutions, shall not become members of political parties.

The membership of the teaching staff at higher education institutions in political parties is regulated by law. This law can not allow those members to assume responsibilities outside the central organs of the political parties. It also sets forth the regulations by which the teaching staff at higher education institutions shall observe as members of political parties.

The State shall provide the political parties with adequate financial means in an equitable manner. The financial assistance to be extended to the political parties, as well as procedures related to collection of membership dues and donations are regulated by law.

B. Principles to be Observed by Political Parties

ARTICLE 69. *(Amended: 23.7.1996 – 4121/7 Article) The activities, internal regulations and operation of political parties shall be in line with democratic principles. The application of these principles is regulated by law.*

Political parties shall not engage in commercial activities.

The income and expenditure of political parties shall be consistent with their objectives. The application of this rule is regulated by law. The auditing of the income and expenditure and acquisitions of political parties as well as the establishment of the conformity to law of their revenue and expenses, methods of auditing and sanctions to be applied in the event of unconformity shall also be regulated by law. The Constitution Court shall be assisted in performing its task of auditing by the Court of Accounts. The judgments to be rendered by the Constitution Court as a result of the auditing shall be final.

The dissolution of political parties shall be decided finally by the Constitutional Court after the filing of a suit by the office of the Chief Public Prosecutor of the Republic.

The permanent dissolution of a political party shall be decided when it is established that the statute and programme of the political party violate the provisions of the fourth paragraph of Article 68.

The decision to dissolve a political party permanently owing to activities violating the provisions of the fourth paragraph of Article 68 may be rendered only when the Constitutional Court determines that the party in question has become a centre for the execution of such activities.

A party which has been dissolved permanently cannot be founded under another name.

The members, including the founders, of a political party whose acts or statements have caused the party to be dissolved permanently cannot be founders, members, directors or supervisors in any other party for a period of five years from the date of publication in the official gazette of the Constitutional Court's final decision and its justification for permanently dissolving the party.

Political parties which accept financial assistance from foreign states, international institutions and persons and corporate bodies shall be dissolved permanently.

The foundation and activities of political parties, their supervision and dissolution, as well as the election expenditures and procedures of the political parties and candidates, are regulated by law in accordance with the above-mentioned principles.

IV. Right to Enter the Public Service

A. Entry into the Public Service

ARTICLE 70. Every Turk has the right to enter the public service.

No criteria other than the qualifications for the office concerned shall be taken into consideration for recruitment into the public service.

B. Declaration of Assets

ARTICLE 71. Declaration of assets by persons entering public service and the frequency of such declaration, shall be determined by law. Those serving in the legislative and executive organs shall not be exempted from this requirement.

V. National Service

ARTICLE 72. National service is the right and duty of every Turk. The manner in which this service shall be performed, or considered as performed, either in the Armed Forces or in the public service shall be regulated by law.

VI. Obligation to Pay Taxes

ARTICLE 73. Everyone is under the obligation to pay taxes according to his financial resources, in order to meet public expenditures.

An equitable and balanced distribution of the tax burden is the social objective of fiscal policy.

Taxes, fees, duties, and other such financial impositions shall be imposed, amended, or revoked by law.

The Council of Ministers may be empowered to amend the percentages of exemption, exceptions and reductions in taxes, feed, duties and other such financial impositions, within the minimum and maximum limits prescribed by law.

VII. Right of Petition

ARTICLE 74. Citizens have the right to apply in writing to the competent authorities and to the Turkish Grand National Assembly with regard to requests and complaints concerning themselves or the public.

The result of the application concerning himself shall be made known to the petitioner in writing.

The way of exercising this right shall be determined by law.

PART THREE

FUNDAMENTAL ORGANS OF THE REPUBLIC

CHAPTER ONE

LEGISLATIVE POWER

I. The Turkish Grand National Assembly

A. Composition

ARTICLE 75. (Amended: 23.7.1995 – 4121/8 Article) The Turkish Grand National Assembly shall be composed of five hundred fifty deputies elected by universal suffrage.

B. Eligibility to Be a Deputy

ARTICLE 76. Every Turk over the age of 30 is eligible to be a deputy.

Persons who have not completed their primary education, who have been deprived of legal capacity, who have failed to perform compulsory military service, who are banned from public service, who have been sentenced to a prison term totaling one year or more excluding involuntary offences, or to a heavy imprisonment; those who have been convicted for dishonourable offences such as embezzlement, corruption, bribery, theft, fraud, forgery, breach of trust, fraudulent bankruptcy; and persons convicted of smuggling, conspiracy in official bidding or purchasing, of offences related to the disclosure of State secrets, of involvement in ideological and anarchistic activities, or incitement and encouragement of such activities, shall not be elected deputies, even if they have been pardoned.

Judges and prosecutors, members of the higher judicial organs, members of the teaching staff at institutions of higher education, members of the Higher Education Council, employees of public institutions and agencies who have the status of civil servants, other public employees not regarded as labourers on account of the duties they perform, and members of the Armed Forces shall not stand for election or be eligible to be a deputy unless they resign from office.

C. Election Term of the Turkish Grand National Assembly

ARTICLE 77. Elections for the Turkish Grand National Assembly shall be held every five years.

If the grounds for deferment do not disappear this measure may be repeated under the procedure for deferment.

By-elections shall be held when vacancies arise in the membership of the Turkish Grand National Assembly. By-elections shall be held once in every election term and cannot be held until 30 months have elapsed from the date of the previous general elections. However, in cases where the number of vacant seats reaches five percent of the total number of seats, by-elections shall be held within three month.

By-elections shall not be held within one year before general elections.

D. General Administration and Supervision of the Elections

ARTICLE 79. Elections shall be held under the general administration and supervision of the judicial organs.

The Supreme Election Council shall execute all the functions to ensure the fair and orderly conduct of the elections from the beginning to the end of polling, carry out investigations and take final decisions on all irregularities, complaints, and objections concerning the elections during and after the polling, and verify the election returns of the members of Turkish Grand National Assembly. No appeal shall be made to any authority against the decisions of the Supreme Election Council.

The functions and powers of the Supreme Election Council and other election councils shall be determined by law.

The Supreme Election Council shall be composed of seven regular members and four substitutes. Six of the members shall be elected by the Plenary Assembly of the High Court of Appeals, and five members shall be elected by the Plenary Assembly of the Council of State from amongst its own members, by secret ballot and by an absolute majority of the total number of members. These members shall elect a Chairman and a Vice-Chairman from amongst themselves, by absolute majority and secret ballot.

Amongst the members elected to the Supreme Election Council by the High Court of Appeals and by the Council of State, two members from each group shall be designated, by lot, as substitute members. The Chairman and Vice-Chairman of the Supreme Election Council shall not take part in this procedure.

The general conduct and supervision of a referendum on legislation amending the Constitution shall be subject to the same provisions as those relating to the election of deputies.

CHAPTER TWO

EXECUTIVE

I. President of the Republic

A. Qualifications and Impartiality

ARTICLE 101. The President of the Republic shall be elected for a term of office of seven years by the Turkish Grand National Assembly from among its own members who are over 40 years of age and who have completed their higher education or from among Turkish citizens who fulfill these requirements and are eligible to be deputies.

The nomination of a candidate for the Presidency of the Republic from outside the Turkish Grand National Assembly shall require a written proposal by a least one-fifth of the total number of members of the Assembly.

The President of the Republic cannot be elected for a second time.

The President-elect, if a member of a party, shall sever his relations with his party, and his status as a member of the Turkish Grand National Assembly shall cease.

B. Election

ARTICLE 102. The President of the Republic shall be elected by a two-thirds majority of the total number of members of the Turkish Grand National Assembly and by secret ballot. If the Turkish Grand National Assembly is not in session, it shall be summoned immediately to meet.

The election of the President of the Republic shall begin thirty days before the term of office of the incumbent President of the Republic expires or ten days after the Presidency fails vacant, and shall be completed within thirty days of the beginning of the election. Candidates shall be declared to the Bureau of the Assembly within the first ten days of this period and elections shall be completed within the remaining twenty days.

If a two-thirds majority of the total number of members cannot be obtained in the first two ballots, between which there shall be at least a three-day interval, a third ballot shall be held and the candidate who receives the absolute majority of votes of the total number of members shall be elected President of the Republic. If an absolute majority of votes of the total number of members is not obtained in the third ballot, a fourth ballot will be held between the two candidates who receive the greatest number of votes in the third ballot; if the President of the Republic cannot be elected by an absolute majority of the total number of members in this ballot, new general elections for the Turkish Grand National Assembly shall be held immediately.

The term of office of the incumbent President of the Republic shall continue until the President-elect takes office.

C. Oath

ARTICLE 103. On assuming office, the President of the Republic shall take the following oath before the Turkish Grand National Assembly:

"In my capacity as President of the Republic I swear upon my honour and integrity before the Turkish Grand National Assembly and before history to safeguard the existence and independence of the State, the indivisible integrity of the Country and the Nation and the absolute sovereignty of the Nation, to abide by the Constitution, the rule of law, democracy, the principles of the secular Republic, not to deviate from the ideal according to which everyone is entitled to enjoy human rights and fundamental freedoms under conditions of national peace and prosperity and in a spirit of national solidarity and justice, and do my utmost to preserve and exalt the glory and honour of the Republic of Turkey and perform without bias the functions that I have assumed."

D. Duties and Powers

ARTICLE 104. The President of the Republic is the Head of the State. In this capacity he/she shall represent the Republic of Turkey and the unity of the Turkish Nation; he/she shall ensure the implementation of the Constitution, and the regular and harmonious functioning of the organs of State.

To this end, the duties he/she shall perform, and the powers he/she shall exercise, in accordance with the conditions stipulated in the relevant articles of the Constitution are as follows:

a) Those relating to legislation:

To deliver, if he/she deems it necessary, the opening address of the Turkish Grand National Assembly on the first day of the legislative year,

To summon the Turkish Grand National Assembly to met, when necessary,

To promulgate laws,

To return laws to the Turkish Grand National Assembly to be reconsidered,

To submit to referendum, if he/she deems it necessary, legislation regarding the amendment of the Constitution.

To appeal to the Constitutional Court for the annulment in part or entirety of certain provisions of laws, decrees having force of law, and the Rules of Procedure of the Turkish Grand National Assembly on the grounds that they are unconstitutional in form or in content,

To call new elections for the Turkish Grand National Assembly.

b) Those relating to the executive functions:

To appoint the Prime Minister and to accept his/her resignation,

To appoint and dismiss Ministers on the proposal of the Prime Minister,

To preside over the Council of Ministers or to call the Council of Ministers to meet under his/her chairmanship whenever he/she deems it necessary,

To accredit representatives of the Turkish State to foreign states to the Republic of Turkey,

To ratify and promulgate international treaties,

To represent the Office of the Commander-in-Chief of the Turkish Armed Forces on behalf of the Turkish Grand National Assembly,

To appoint the Chief of the General Staff,

To call the National Security Council to meet,

To preside over the National Security Council to meet.

To proclaim martial law or state of emergency, and to issue decrees having force of law, in accordance with the decisions of the Council of Ministers under his/her chairmanship,

To sign decrees,

To remit, on grounds of chronic illness, disability, or old age, all or part of the sentences imposed on certain individuals,

To appoint the members and the chairman of the State Supervisory Council,

To instruct the State Supervisory Council to carry out inquiries, investigations and inspections,

To appoint the members of the Higher Education Council,

To appoint rectors of universities.

c) Those relating to the judiciary:

To appoint the members of the Constitution Court, one-fourth of the members of the Council of State, the Chief Public Prosecutor and the Deputy Chief Public Prosecutor of the High Court of Appeals, the members of the Military High Court of Appeals, the members of the Supreme Military Administrative Court and the members of the Supreme Council of Judges and Public Prosecutors.

The President of the Republic shall also exercise powers of election and appointment, and perform the other duties conferred on him by the Constitution and laws.

PART THREE

JUDICIAL POWER

I. General Provisions

A. Independence of the Courts

ARTICLE 138. Judges shall be independent in the discharge of their duties; they shall give judgment in accordance with the Constitution, law, and their personal conviction conforming with the law.

No organ, authority, office or individual may give orders or instructions to courts or judges relating to the exercise of judicial power, send them circulars, or make recommendations or suggestions.

No questions shall be asked, debates held, or statements made in the Legislative Assembly relating to the exercise of judicial power concerning a case under trial.

Legislative and executive organs and the administration shall comply with court decisions; these organs and the administration shall neither alter them in any respect, nor delay their execution.

B. Security of Tenure of Judges and Public Prosecutors

ARTICLE 139. Judges and public prosecutors shall not be dismissed, or retired before the age prescribed by the Constitution; nor shall they be deprived of their salaries, allowances or other rights relating to their status, even as a result of the abolition of court or post.

Exceptions indicated in law relating to those convicted for an offence requiring dismissal from the profession, those who are definitely established as unable to perform their duties on account of ill-health, and those determined as unsuitable to remain in the profession, are reserved.

C. Judges and Public Prosecutors

ARTICLE 140. Judges and public prosecutors shall serve as judges and public prosecutors or courts of justice and of administrative courts. These duties shall be carried out by career judges and public prosecutors.

Judges shall discharge their duties in accordance with the principles of the independence of the courts and the security of tenure of judges.

The qualifications, appointment, rights and duties, salaries and allowances of judges and public prosecutors, their promotion, temporary or permanent change in their duties or posts, the initiation of disciplinary proceedings against them and the subsequent imposition of disciplinary penalties, the conduct of investigation concerning them and the subsequent decision to prosecute them on account of offences committed in connection with, or in the course of, their duties, the conviction for offences or instances of incompetence requiring their dismissal from the profession, their in-service training and other matters relating to their personnel status shall be regulated by law in accordance with the principles of the independence of the courts and the security of tenure of judges.

Judges and public prosecutors shall exercise their duties until they reach the age of sixty-five; the promotion according to age and the retirement of military judges shall be prescribed by law.

Judges and public prosecutors shall not assume official or public functions other than those prescribed by law.

Judges and public prosecutors shall be attached to the Ministry of justice in so far as their administrative functions are concerned.

Those judges and public prosecutors working in administrative posts of the justice service shall be subject to the same provisions as other judges and public prosecutors. Their categories and grades shall be determined according to the principles applying to judges and public prosecutors and they shall enjoy all the rights accorded to judges and public prosecutors.

D. Publicity of Hearings and Verdict Justification

ARTICLE 141. Court hearings shall be open to the public. It may be decided to conduct all or part of the hearings in closed session only in cases where absolutely required for reasons of public morality or public security.

Special provisions shall be provided in the law with respect to the trial of minors.

The decisions of all courts shall be made in writing with a statement of justification.

It is the duty of the judiciary to conclude trials as quickly as possible and at minimum cost.

E. Organization of Courts

ARTICLE 142. The organization, functions, and jurisdiction of the courts, their functioning and trial procedures shall be regulated by law.

BIBLIOGRAPHY

Bailyn, Bernard. *The Ideological Origins of the American Revolution.* Cambridge: Harvard University Press, 1967.

Douglass, David C., editor. *English Historical Documents.* 12 vols. Oxford: Oxford University Press, 1950–1968.

Diggins, John. *The Lost Soul of American Politics.* New York: Basic, 1984.

Jefferson, Thomas and Adams, John. *The Adams-Jefferson Letters.* 2 vols. Edited by Lester Cappon. Chapel Hill: University of North Carolina Press, 1959.

Jefferson, Thomas. *Autobiography.* New York: Putnam.

Jefferson, Thomas. *The Papers of Thomas Jefferson.* 30 vols. Edited by Julian boyd. Princeton: Princeton University Press, 1950–1998.

Jefferson, Thomas. *The Writings of Thomas Jefferson.* 20 vols. Edited by Albert Ellery Bergh. Washington, D.C.: Thomas Jefferson Memorial Association, 1904–1905.

Jefferson. Thomas. *The Complete Jefferson.* Edited by Saul K. Padover. New York: Tudor, 1943.

Kinross, Patrick. *Atatürk: The Birth of a Nation.* London: Weidenfeld, 1964.

Knorr, Klaus. *British Colonial Theories 1570–1850.* Toronto: University of Toronto Press, 1944.

Koebner, Richard. *Empire.* Cambridge: Cambridge University Press, 1961.

Kramnick, Isaac. *Bolingbroke and His Circle.* Cambridge: Harvard University Press, 1968.

Locke, John. *Treatises of Government.* Edited by Peter Laslett. New York: New American Library, 1965.

McCoy, Drew. *The Elusive Republic.* Chapel Hill: University of North Carolina Press, 1980.

Morison, Samuel Eliot. *The Oxford History of the American People.* Vol. 3. New York: Mentor, 1972.

Nation, Mastneyt. *Turkey: Between East and West.* Boulder: Westview Press, 1996.

Ozel, Mehmet. *Atatürk.* Ankara: Ajans-Turk, 1991.

Peterson, Merrill. *Thomas Jefferson and the New Nation.* New York: Oxford University Press, 1970.

Pocock, J. G. A. *The Ancient Constitution and the Feudal Law*. Cambridge: Cambridge University Press, 1957.

Pocock, J. G. A. *Virtue, Commerce and History*. Cambridge: Cambridge University Press, 1985.

Roeber, A. G. *Faithful Magistrates and Republican Lawyers*. Chapel Hill: University of North Carolina Press, 1981.

Rose, J. Holland, et al. editors. *The Cambridge History of the British Empire*. Cambridge: Cambridge University Press, 1929.

Sanford, Charles B. *The Religious Life of Thomas Jefferson*. Charlottesville: University Press of Virginia, 1984.

Sheldon, Garrett Ward. *The Political Philosophy of Thomas Jefferson*. Baltimore: Johns Hopkins University Press, 1991.

Sheldon, Garrett Ward. *What Would Jefferson Say?* New York: Penguin, 1998.

Wills, Garry. *Inventing America: Jefferson's Declaration of Independence*. New York: Doubleday, 1978.

INDEX

Major Concepts in Politics and Political Theory

This series invites book manuscripts and proposals on major concepts in politics and political theory—justice, equality, virtue, rights, citizenship, power, sovereignty, property, liberty, etc.—in prominent traditions, periods, and thinkers.

Send manuscripts or proposals, with author's vitae to:

Garrett Ward Sheldon
General Editor
Clinch Valley College
of the University of Virginia
College Avenue
Wise, VA 24293

To order other books in this series, please contact our Customer Service Department:

(800) 770-LANG (within the U.S.)
(212) 647-7706 (outside the U.S.)
(212) 647-7707 FAX

Or browse online by series at:

www.peterlang.com